Barbara Victor

THE LADY

BARBARA VICTOR is a journalist who has covered the Middle East for most of her career. She is also the author of four novels, which have been translated into twenty-two languages, and six nonfiction works, including a biography of Madonna, *Goddess: Inside Madonna*, which was an international best-seller. Her most recent nonfiction work is *Women Suicide Bombers*, which will coincide with her television film documentary on women suicide bombers in the Occupied Territories and Gaza. Ms. Victor and her husband divide their time between Paris and New York.

Also by Barbara Victor

Getting Away With Murder

Voice of Reason: Hanan Ashrawi and Peace in the Middle East

Coriander

Friends, Lovers, Enemies

Misplaced Lives

Absence of Pain

Terrorism

Le Matignon de Jospin

Goddess: Inside Madonna

THE LADY

AUNG SAN SUU KYI:
NOBEL LAUREATE AND BURMA'S PRISONER

BARBARA VICTOR

Faber and Faber, Inc.
An affiliate of Farrar, Straus and Giroux
New York

My gratitude to all those who were so generous with their time and knowledge in helping me with my research for this book. Unfortunately, given the political situation that exists in Burma, it is impossible to cite any of those people by name as they fear for either their jobs, their political future, or simply their lives.

Faber and Faber, Inc.
An affiliate of Farrar, Straus and Giroux
19 Union Square West, New York 10003

Copyright © 1998 by Barbara Victor
Afterword copyright © 2002 by Barbara Victor
All rights reserved
Distributed in Canada by Penguin Books of Canada Limited
Printed in the United States of America
Published in 1998 by Faber and Faber, Inc.
First paperback edition, 2002

The Library of Congress has cataloged the hardcover edition as follows:
Victor, Barbara.
    The lady : Aung San Suu Kyi: Nobel Laureate and Burma's Prisoner /
Barbara Victor.
        p.   cm.
    ISBN 0-571-19944-5
    1. Aung San Suu Kyi. 2. Women political activists—Burma—Biography.
3. Women political prisoners—Burma—Biography. 4. Political
Corruption—Burma. 5. Political ethics—Burma. 6. Burma—Politics and
government. I. Title.
HQ1735.7.Z75A859   1998
959.1054092-dc21
[B]   97-47042
                                                                   CIP

Paperback ISBN: 0-571-21177-1

Designed by Will Powers

www.fsgbooks.com

1 3 5 7 9 10 8 6 4 2

THE LADY

1

O N   T H E   S U R F A C E, Rangoon, or *Yangon* as it has been renamed by the Burmese military government, looks like
any other overcrowded city in Southeast Asia.

On a typical rush-hour morning, broken-down buses weave
through the traffic, with people clinging to the sides and roof or
hanging from the windows. Purchased from the Israelis in 1948
and never refitted for new emission systems, the buses leave
clouds of pollution in their wake.

At various intervals along the sidewalks, soda bottles filled
with gasoline are set on small piles of bricks, the Burmese version of a filling station. The official price of gas sold at government pumps is 25 *kyats* (Burmese currency) a gallon, while the
black market price is 350 kyats a gallon. With the exception of
certain government workers and foreigners, the Burmese are allowed only four gallons per week, forcing them to buy gasoline
by the bottle rather than by the gallon. Garbage collection for
the rich (government workers and foreigners) is also cheaper and
more efficient than it is for most Burmese: bins of trash in poor
neighborhoods often sit uncollected for days or even weeks.

On the main thoroughfares leading to the more upscale
neighborhoods in Rangoon, monks clad in flowing orange robes
walk in single file. Carrying begging bowls, they stop next to
steaming cauldrons of rice and fish that the faithful wait to serve

them every morning. Nearby, along the sidewalks, *trishaw* drivers linger under the shade of banyan trees, chatting idly as they watch the stream of humanity begin another day.

The disparity between rich and poor is found throughout the country, with the majority of the population living in terrible squalor, without proper food, sanitary conditions, shelter, or medical care. Basic services in Rangoon, however, are equally inefficient for everyone. Even in the best hotels the tap water is undrinkable, the plumbing barely functions, and electricity is grossly inadequate for the massive construction that is going on. Blackouts occur every day and last anywhere from five minutes to five hours, causing havoc with all the high-tech office machines in the burgeoning business community. As for paved roads, the surfaces usually crack within months under the heat of the scorching sun, leaving gaping holes and causing numerous traffic accidents.

Rangoon is atypical of the rest of the country, as is evident in the various styles of architecture—another example of the contrast between rich and poor. A plethora of luxury hotels has recently been constructed downtown in anticipation that the city will become a mecca for tourism and international business. Farther along toward the Rangoon River, shabby colonial-style buildings with wide verandas still stand, built during British rule when Burma was presented to Queen Victoria as a New Year's present. Behind them on narrow unpaved streets, pockets of squatters' huts and run-down apartment houses are crammed together, resembling projects in the worst inner-city slums. Children play in alleyways filled with sewage, while nearby, under makeshift stands, their parents hawk everything from cheap souvenirs and magazines to soap powder and toothpaste.

Certain areas of Rangoon have stores and minimalls that appear to overflow with consumer goods, as well as luxury items such as perfume, whiskey, wine, and cosmetics. Prices are high, however, which makes the products accessible only to foreigners or those privileged Burmese who are allowed to keep dollar accounts.

According to a report by the United States Department of State, called *Foreign Economic Trends in Burma* and published in June 1996,

> The government of Burma, from 1990 through 1994, reduced the scope of public sector imports for private sector consumption and phased out subsidies reflecting the official exchange rate. In 1990, when the regime began to liberalize external trade, they allowed exporters to hold dollar-dominated accounts in domestic banks, allowed such dollars to be traded legally for *kyat* at parallel exchange rates . . . although these dollar deposits could be used to purchase imports, they could be converted at the market rate only to purchase local goods for export, not for domestic consumption.

In February 1993, the government introduced a form of local currency pegged to the U.S. dollar, called the foreign exchange certificate, or FEC. Only foreign-currency holders, however, including tourists and exporters, could exchange dollars for FEC at the market-determined parallel rate to buy local goods and services. By 1995, hardly any transactions except intra-public-sector transactions and tax transactions still occurred at prices reflecting the official exchange rate.

Continuing toward downtown Rangoon in the direction of the British and American embassies are modern high-rise residential buildings in varying stages of completion, all designed with sweeping driveways and manicured lawns leading to their entrances. Directly northeast of downtown Rangoon, through the winding tree-lined roads with views of the Shwedagon Pagoda, past the opulent stucco homes that were built by the British, is a large artificial body of water called Inya Lake. As investment pours into Burma, or *Myanmar* as it has been renamed by the military government, and western businessmen and their families take up temporary residence in Rangoon, the lake has become a popular weekend spot.

On the southern shore of Inya Lake is the Myanmar Sailing Club, which sponsors regular races as well as the prestigious annual Regatta, and the Yangon Arts and Science University that has some of the most modern architecture in all of Rangoon. Scattered along the shore of the lake are government guest houses and ministerial mansions, most of which are off-limits to the general public. Also bordering Inya Lake is the American diplomatic residential compound, a cluster of neat placard houses where the general staff live, and where several grander colonial mansions are reserved for the United States Ambassador and the Chargé d'Affaires. Guarded by an electric gate that is usually left unarmed and open, and a sentry booth manned by local Burmese with neither guns nor shoes, the compound is off-limits to everyone except residents and their invited guests. Since 1990, in a gesture of disapproval of the current military regime, the house reserved for the American Ambassador remains unoccupied.

On the opposite side of Inya Lake is another compound, surrounded by an electrified steel fence and, rumor has it, land mines buried on the grounds, along with two thousand troops on duty at all times. On a clear night searchlights are visible, sweeping over the murky waters, as boats patrol the shore in front of the house. It is there that General Ne Win lives, the retired dictator who ruled Burma for more than two decades with a mixture of xenophobia, paranoia, astrology, and a smattering of both Buddhism and Marxism.

Despite a palpable climate of fear that permeates the country and the government spies and informers who mingle among the people, the atmosphere around the lake is usually carefree. On most mornings, before the heat becomes oppressive, many Burmese jog or power walk on the cement paths built along its banks. Groups of older men and women, wrapped in the traditional sarongs or *longyis*, with rubber sandals flapping against the pavement, also gather to exercise and socialize before the day begins. The younger set, attired in the latest jogging clothes and sneakers, take their morning workouts more seriously. The most popular jogging route is a one-kilometer path that runs between the International Business Center, yet another newly constructed glass office building, and a roadside restaurant set in a muddy terrain, which features fish and noodles brewing over an open fire.

At the end of the day, the shores of Inya Lake are crowded once again with people who gather to enjoy the beauty of the pink, blue, and white lotuses that float on the lake's surface, or to watch the golden sun as it sets in the indigo-blue Burmese sky.

Before 1988, the Inya Lake Hotel was the most famous structure on the lake. Originally constructed by the Soviets in the 1960s, it was a dreary, gray, stone, box-like building, typical of the drab architectural style that the communists put up all over Eastern Europe. Recently the hotel has been completely renovated and refurbished due to a Hong Kong investment of more than $6 million. But while it is now considered one of the most luxurious tourist havens in Rangoon, its most-famous-structure status has been usurped by another house that is situated directly across Inya Lake from General Ne Win's compound.

Set in the middle of a ragged garden of overgrown grass, weeds, and flowers, that two-story villa is in a state of crumbling ruin. Surrounded by a blue wood fence on which flags and banners hang—green figures of dancing peacocks painted on simple white discs—the house has come to symbolize the Burmese pro-democracy movement. Unlike the Inya Lake Hotel, however, the building is known less for its architecture than it is for its owner.

She is Daw Aung San Suu Kyi, the fifty-two-year-old Nobel Peace Prize laureate and the most well-known political dissident since Nelson Mandela was released from a South African prison.

In Burma, Aung San Suu Kyi is almost always referred to as "The Lady." It is a respectful title bestowed on her by the people who are reluctant to mention her name out loud for fear of reprisal by the military regime, called the State Law and Order Restoration Council, and better known by its Orwellian acronym, the SLORC. Curiously, the SLORC also refers to Aung San Suu Kyi as The Lady, less out of deference, however, than to avoid mentioning the name of her famous father, General Aung San, who in 1947 negotiated Burma's independence from the British. Considered to be the Burmese equivalent of George Washington, and credited with founding the *Tatmadaw,* or Burmese Army, General Aung San also became the country's most famous martyr when assassins' bullets ended his life only months before he was to become the first leader of the new independent state. Given the image of respect and honor that accompanies General Aung San's name, the SLORC is loathe to add any more prestige to his daughter, a woman who has already garnered the love and respect of the Burmese people.

In September 1996, I traveled to Burma for the first time and stayed for two months. On that particular visit I had an official visa, and permission from the SLORC to do research. In fact, the SLORC arranged my accommodations in advance in a large guest house, owned and operated by the Directorate of Defense Services Intelligence.

My room was large, furnished in expensive teak and crushed velvet upholstered chairs and couches, with a four-poster antique bed, a beveled-glass china cabinet, color television with cable, and refrigerator. All my windows had views of a swimming pool, and from a large veranda I could see the dome of the Shwedagon Pagoda. Later on, I discovered that there were also several listening devices planted in an overhead chandelier in my room and along the floorboards near my bed.

Before I left for Burma, the SLORC set down two conditions. They would agree to let me interview high-ranking military leaders and former drug czars, as well as academics and business people, on the condition that I write an unbiased and fair book. The second condition was that I could travel outside Rangoon—accompanied by a military escort—if I agreed *not* to contact The Lady, or anyone else from what the government referred to as the "political opposition." If I agreed, the SLORC informed me, I would be able to "see for myself" all the economic and social progress the regime was making, and be the first to "tell the world the real story about Myanmar."

From its inception, the SLORC's bargain was disturbing.

First of all, the fact that they referred to Aung San Suu Kyi and other pro-democracy advocates as the "opposition" was erroneous. The reality is that the National League for Democracy party, called the NLD, of which Aung San Suu Kyi is a founding member, had legitimately won 82 percent of the popular vote in free elections that had been organized by the SLORC in 1990. The regime chose not to recognize those election results, which made *them* the "opposition" at the very least, and more accurately, a brutal military junta that took over the country by force and continues to use brutal measures to remain in power.

The second part of the bargain had to do with what the SLORC meant by a "fair and unbiased" book. Restricting me in what I could see or where I could go in the country on my own to research, and preventing me from interviewing anyone I believed could add something to the book, was unacceptable. My intention was to talk with as many people as possible—including Aung San Suu Kyi, as well as other members of the NLD, along with ordinary Burmese who had been victims of the regime in one way or another.

During the two months that I spent in Burma on that initial trip, a colonel was assigned to organize my daily schedule and set up all my interviews. It was with Colonel Hla Min, a high-ranking military official attached to the Defense Ministry and also one of the principal advisors to General Khin Nyunt, who is known as Secretary One and is the man who most Burmese believe is the main brains behind the current regime, that I negotiated the SLORC's conditions.

Educated in the United States as a child and adolescent during his father's tenure as the Burmese ambassador to Washington, Colonel Hla Min spoke flawless English, was well-versed in American slang, loved baseball, and apparently had a good idea of what effective western public relations was all about. As a result, in typical convoluted SLORC logic, the Colonel announced that "for my own safety," while they would not give me permission to talk to "dangerous dissidents," they would not stop me provided that I took responsibility for anything that happened to me when I was not with my government minder. In the end, we came to a tacit understanding—something like "don't ask,

don't tell"—which meant that at the whim of the SLORC, my research could be confiscated and I could be thrown out of the
country.

From that day on, after every meeting that I arranged on my
own, Colonel Hla Min would wander down to the guest house
and engage me in casual conversation. It was obvious that these
visits were all an effort to refute the negative reports that, he
rightly assumed, I had heard about the government.

2

SPEND ANY TIME IN RANGOON and it is obvious that the city operates almost entirely on rumor. Travel around Burma and it is obvious that the country functions almost entirely on contradiction.

Some say that word of mouth has become the most dependable way of communicating because the infrastructure is so lacking in modern equipment and technology. Others claim that the Burmese penchant for inventing or reinventing various versions of the truth has to do with the people's profound belief in astrology. Almost every Burmese, including members of the SLORC, consults a favorite nun or monk, spiritualist, or astrologer for advice on handling love, life, health, or business problems, as well as forecasting the future. Given this unorthodox way that the Burmese run their lives and their country, it is no wonder that outside nations or human-rights groups, trying to grasp political patterns and trends in Burma, find themselves unable to separate fact from propaganda, reality from illusion. What is certain in Burma is that interpreting signs, numbers, and symbols as a way of understanding political events is more reliable than depending on the SLORC, which censors and suppresses information.

Putting aside the stars and planets as a means of communicating for the moment, the more usual infrastructure is yet another example of the inherent contradiction found throughout the country. Although the telephone lines are inadequate and archaic, the SLORC has nonetheless succeeded in creating a system of surveillance that is unsurpassed in the scope of its intrusiveness. Telephones in all diplomatic residences and hotels are tapped, while telephones of known pro-democracy party members and others in opposition to the regime are not only tapped, but the lines are also cut intermittently, without warning. The chief censoring body of the media is the Press Scrutiny Board, which accounts for the limited international news in the country's official newspaper, *The New Light of Myanmar*, and which also censors all references within the country to poverty, bribery, and corruption.

The overall pervasive security apparatus that enables the SLORC to keep its tight control over the population is called the Directorate of Defense Services Intelligence, or DDSI, which has interests in several real estate ventures in Rangoon. Control is buttressed by restrictions on contact with foreigners, surveillance of government employees as well as private citizens, harassment of political activists, and intimidation, arrest, detention, and physical abuse.

Given the infrastructure and censorship, it is no wonder that most people living in Rangoon don't have firsthand knowledge of the conditions in Mandalay, for instance, a city that is only a few hundred kilometers away. Nor does the average citizen hear of the many human-rights abuses and forced labor that are occurring in the surrounding rural areas, especially ethnic minority regions where armed opposition movements have been fighting against the central government since independence. As for traveling within the country, with the exception of certain VIP foreigners and tourists, the SLORC has set down stringent rules prohibiting anyone, including the diplomatic community, from venturing more than twenty-five kilometers out of any city without special permission or registration. In its own defense, the SLORC admits that it curtails trips to outlying areas for reasons of security. "There are armed groups of rebels and insurgents,"

Colonel Hla Min explained to me. "We are only trying to protect visitors as well as our own Myanmar citizens from being injured or killed."

According to Donald Keyser, who is the director of the Office of Asia, Africa, Europe, and Multilateral Programs at the Bureau of International Narcotics and Law Enforcement, United States Department of State, "The SLORC are forced to hold onto that Big Brother society by using a very pervasive intelligence apparatus because it's the only way to maintain national security and unity."

There are other, less sophisticated, surveillance measures that the SLORC uses as well, such as paid informers who trail behind foreigners, especially journalists and diplomats, either in cars or on foot, eavesdropping on their conversations and reporting on their daily activities.

On a tourist outing to the Shwedagon Pagoda one day, in the company of the wife of a high-ranking American diplomat, we experienced an unpleasant but almost comical example of how Burma, under the current military regime, has become Orwellian.

A young Burmese woman, heavily pregnant, was on her knees in the scorching sun, diligently cleaning an entire wall of a pagoda with a small brush. Kneeling down next to her, my companion asked in Burmese how much she earned for her work. At that moment, a young Burmese man, wearing a *longyi* and a white shirt, wraparound sunglasses shielding his face, and carrying a black attaché case, sprinted forward until he was practically on top of us. Crouching down beside my companion and the Burmese woman without any effort to be discrete, he proceeded to eavesdrop on their conversation. After several minutes, when the man was apparently satisfied that he had heard enough, he sprinted away, disappearing into the maze of Buddhas, pagodas, and shrines.

Later on, we asked a member of Aung San Suu Kyi's political party what the repercussions could be for the young woman who answered my companion's question. "As long as she only answered the question," we were told, "telling what she earned without complaining, she might get a stern lecture from the authorities." Then he added, "Had she complained or talked against the SLORC, it is likely that she would be imprisoned."

*　*　*

There are numerous splendors throughout Burma. Every year thousands of tourists admire the natural beauties of the country, such as the lush green forests and exotic flowers, or visit the many pagodas with golden domes encrusted with precious jewels that glimmer on their peaks, or wander the open-air markets that sell everything from gemstones to Japanese stereos, local artifacts to spices. Since 1988, however, when Aung San Suu Kyi became internationally recognized as the voice of democracy, her rambling, run-down villa has become the country's most visited, talked-about, and photographed attraction. As the headquarters of the National League for Democracy party, the house itself has become an oasis of democracy and freedom in one of the most oppressed countries in the world.

Fox Television in the United States asked me to shoot some footage of the country, as well as film several interviews I would be conducting of its leaders. The local television crew that I hired happened to be under the direction of Colonel Hla Min's brother.

On an excursion to visit a satellite city several kilometers outside Rangoon, I was taken to what was described by my government guides as one example of several suburban communities that were under construction for the "burgeoning middle class." Ranging in price from $30,000 to $60,000, the four model homes that I was shown in that particular suburban community had, according to my guides, all been sold to families in Rangoon who decided to try "life in the new suburbs."

On the way from one area to the other, we passed an entire section of undeveloped swamp land where huts built on stilts stood in the murky waters. Children of all ages played in the mud while, inside the huts, pigs sprawled on dirt floors next to mats where the family slept. One hand-pump supplied potable water for the entire community that had thirty-five to fifty families each comprised of at least six or seven people.

Serge Pun is the chairman of SPA International Limited, a Hong Kong company engaged in a joint financial venture with the SLORC to build those particular satellite cities. Mr. Pun told me that the people who lived in those huts on the periphery of the construction sites were employed as construction workers. "These people are itinerant workers who travel from construction site to construction site around the country," Pun explained. "Most of them would die of starvation if it weren't for the progress being made by the SLORC, and the fact that there are numerous construction projects like this one throughout the country."

In answer to questions concerning schools and medical facilities for those workers, the government guide gestured somewhere in the distance. "There are schools and medical facilities available for everyone," he assured me. When I asked to be taken to one of those facilities, my host suggested that a tour of a nearby bread factory would give me a better understanding of the government's progress in reducing the unemployment level.

As for the SLORC's claim of a "burgeoning middle class," it was unclear what they meant. The average teacher earns the equivalent of $30 per month, which is why many have quit the profession to work privately, many as traders but some even in the jade and ruby mines in the mountains of the far northeast. It seemed unlikely that someone in that salary range could afford a house that cost $30,000. As one former teacher explained to me several days later, "Very few people could pay that much for a house." She smiled. "At least by working in the jade mines, we earn enough to feed our families."

Those who still teach often have second jobs, either as private tutors or in blue-collar professions where they are paid in cash. Still others, mostly those who teach at Yangon University and who are driven to desperate measures to pay rents in Rangoon—

which are higher than their monthly salaries—have taken to charging parents and/or students "fees" to be allowed to sit in their classes and take exams.

According to a report on human-rights practices in Burma compiled by the United States government in 1996, "only government employees and employees of a few traditional industries are covered by minimum wage provisions. The minimum monthly wage for salaried public employees is $5.00, but that sum is supplemented by various subsidies and allowances. Under ordinary circumstances, the minimum wage is insufficient to provide a decent standard of living for a worker and family, and usually fosters widespread corruption."

While foreign governments and human-rights groups claim that the fear throughout Burma is almost tangible, advocates for the SLORC counterclaim that the people have never been better off, that there is an increase in jobs and an overall climate of real economic growth that has raised the standard of living. Concerning all the construction that is going on in Rangoon, or "progress" as the SLORC prefers to call it, Aung San Suu Kyi has this to say: "If the government really wanted to help Burma they should think of the broader human development of the country rather than economic development in narrow terms of more investments, tourists, and hotels. I would like to see new schools, new hospitals, new nurseries, new libraries, new bookshops."

When I finished shooting for Fox, the Colonel's brother sat with me in an edit room. Most of the damaging images that I had managed to capture on tape ended up on the cutting room floor. In an effort to placate me, however, Colonel Hla Min trotted out "Mr. and Mrs. Average Burmese Citizen," "the man on the street," countless "ordinary people," he claimed, whom I could interview—always in his presence—and who would, not surprisingly, recite words of praise for the regime and negative comments about Aung San Suu Kyi.

"The Lady is hurting the country," one person told me in front of Colonel Hla Min. "She calls for sanctions that take the food out of the mouths of our children." Another proclaimed,

"Aung San Suu Kyi blocks progress in Myanmar, while her own family lives in the lap of luxury in England."

Tourists and visitors who come to Burma are frequently blinded by the natural beauty of the country, misled by the multi-million-dollar foreign investment projects in various stages of completion, fooled by the friendly and polite Burmese, and unaware that even the exchange rate available to them is far more advantageous than the rate available to the average Burmese. For example, the official exchange rate is six kyats to the dollar, while the black market rate has fluctuated in recent years between 100 and 280 kyats to the dollar. Yet the ordinary citizen struggling to make ends meet is forbidden, under penalty of prison, to engage in any illegal black market money exchange. According to the report *Foreign Economic Trends in Burma,* published in June 1996 by the United States Department of State, since 1990 the government of Burma has "implemented a gradual and now largely complete liberalization of the exchange rate regime, in many respects tantamount to a *de facto* devaluation of the kyat."

Since 1990, the country's rampant inflation has made it impossible for the average Burmese to have enough to eat. In the past seven years, under the SLORC, the price of chicken, for instance, went from 100 kyats to 400 kyats for about 1.6 kilograms, while pork went from 70 kyats to 280 per 1.6 kilograms. Even the price of *mohinga*, a typical fish broth that cost 3 kyats a bowl before 1990, now costs 15 kyats for a smaller portion. When I pointed this out to Colonel Hla Min, his response was, "The Myanmar people have never been hungry. We could close up the country for another twenty years and the people would never starve."

Given the rich soil and numerous natural resources, it would indeed be difficult to starve. Yet there is a vast difference between starving and not knowing where the next meal is coming from.

Douglas Rasmussen, the American Counselor for Political and Economic Affairs at the United States Embassy in Rangoon, states that "For decades, Burma has been a subsistence economy.

The tragedy is that the country has the potential to be rich. In fact, before General Ne Win came to power in 1962, Burma was the rice-basket of Southeast Asia. By the time he left, Burma was one of the poorest countries in the world."

The Burmese people are getting poorer and living in more and more desperate circumstances, while the SLORC is getting richer and, as a result, intensifying its stranglehold on the country. Daw Suu Kyi explains one aspect of that control. "One of the ways the government tries to stop people from being involved in the democracy movement is to encourage them to take an interest in business and not in politics. That is, if you are concentrated on just making money in this country you have to indulge in a lot of things that are—not quite strict. There is a lot of bribery and corruption going on. You do lose the morality if you are told to concentrate only on making money and if you are made to feel that as long as you are making money, you won't get into trouble. So, people think that it's much more dangerous to support the democracy movement than to bribe someone."

Another major source of corruption in Burma involves the SLORC's claims that they have programs to eradicate poppy and opium crops and, therefore, curtail heroin traffic to western nations. The government arranged an interview with several government workers involved in the eradication of poppy, as well as a drug lord who had given up the profession. Curiously, they all told me that Buddhism was the reason opium production had been curtailed—because it had a negative affect on the world.

I spent a great deal of time with several anti-narcotic experts based in foreign embassies who had been sent to Rangoon, ostensibly to work with the SLORC in combatting the drug problem. According to them, and to several official reports written by the United States Department of State, Burma remains the largest exporter of opium in the Golden Triangle, shipping through Laos, Thailand, and China to major western cities.

One of the SLORC's major complaints is that the United States has stopped giving financial support to help the Burmese government solve the drug problem. Robert S. Gelbard, during his tenure as the United States Assistant Secretary of State for International Narcotics and Law-Enforcement Affairs, accused the SLORC of "turning a blind eye to drug producers, and running money-laundering operations, as well as profiting directly from the trade." Gelbard has since left his job for another within the Department of State. Some observers believe that General Barry McCaffrey, the director of the United States Office of National Drug Control Policy, will be taking a more active role in shaping American policy toward drug eradication in Burma. Shortly before assuming his position last year, McCaffrey summed up Washington's confusion. "It is not clear to me," McCaffrey said, "what the U.S. will do because for the present, the dominant concern is . . . the human-rights situation confronting the Burmese people. And I don't know where we will go." General McCaffrey's dilemma is shared by a large part of the international community.

Spending time in Burma gives one the impression that the country is no different than any country under occupation, similar even to the Occupied Territories in the Middle East. The fact that Burma's occupiers happen to be Burmese and not a foreign entity does nothing to change the end result. The SLORC as occupiers have stripped the country not only of its natural resources, but have also confiscated the people's homes and land, as well as denied them their freedom and basic human-rights. The only similarity between the twenty-two members of the SLORC and the rest of the Burmese population is a common history and language.

Without exception, outside investors who do business in Burma—ventures that range from real estate to drug trafficking to money laundering—are selected based on their understanding and agreement that all profits are shared with the SLORC. Although kickbacks and bribes are not unusual, what is most disturbing is how many foreigners who represent legitimate enterprises—both Asians and westerners—and who may well be moral and upstanding citizens in their own countries, change drastically when they arrive in Burma. Somehow, they tend to ignore all the basic tenets of human-rights. Instead of bringing with them their own code of ethics, they embrace the practices of the SLORC and pay the Burmese shamefully low wages; frequently turn a blind eye to inhuman conditions without proper breaks for food, shade, or water; and tacitly condone the razing of people's homes and lands to make way for their companies' industrial projects. The higher the financial gain, the more blinded these foreign investors and businessmen are to any international standards of decency and human-rights.

It is a cruel equation.

3

G ENERAL MAUNG MAUNG, the Secretary of the Foreign
Investment Commission, had a very precise message for
me at the beginning of my trip. The world, especially the United
States, was spreading false information about Myanmar. As an
example, he cited a visit by United States Secretary of State
Madeleine Albright when she was the American Ambassador to
the United Nations. According to General Maung Maung, during that particular visit, Secretary Albright made the comment
that the Burmese people smiled all the time to cover up their
fear. How ridiculous, General Maung Maung laughed, "the Burmese people smile because they are happy," he told me. "Their
life is good under the SLORC."

Unfortunately, Secretary Albright's observation was not
wrong. The Burmese people, while naturally charming and
friendly, also have an amazing facility for talking with their eyes.
In Rangoon I became familiar with the constant smiles that were
frozen on the people's lips, and all too aware that their eyes told
quite another story.

When I asked the masseuse, who came unannounced each
morning to administer a massage that lasted for one hour and
cost $3, if life has improved under the SLORC, she pointed
around the room before putting a finger to her lips. When I
inquired of the driver assigned to me who sat and waited, often

for hours, even if he wasn't needed, and who earned less than $25 for twelve- and fifteen-hour workdays, if the economy was booming, his answer was that things have never been better. When I asked him specifics, however, about feeding his family, educating his children, and the possibility of speaking out against the regime, the expression in his eyes belied his smile and his words of praise for the military.

When I quizzed the woman who functioned as my minder if it was true that people are dragged from their homes and forced to build railroad tracks, or work on infrastructure projects related to the multi-million-dollar Yadana gas pipeline currently under construction in the southern part of the country, I heard the following explanation. "It is the Buddhist way. Our people are only too proud to contribute their labor for the good of the country. If a rural village needs a railroad to ship crops to the cities, the government will supply the material and the village head will supply the labor. Since any improvement like a bridge or railroad is for the good of the village, the people are only too happy to work without pay since it will improve their lives."

When I asked her about the thousands of Burmese in the rural areas, mostly ethnic minorities, who are forced by armed soldiers to leave their villages to be relocated to unfamiliar areas, she replied, "The conditions of some of the villages are uninhabitable and Secretary One [the common name given to General Khin Nyunt, who is the SLORC's main strategist] is only trying to improve the standard of living."

When I wondered about villagers or certain ethnic minorities who are rounded up at random and used by the army as human land-mine sweepers, or porters made to carry inordinately heavy loads, my minder admonished me by saying, "Aung San Suu Kyi's pro-democracy movement is responsible for those ugly rumors because she wants to hurt the country." And, when I suggested that the people love The Lady and fear the SLORC, she replied, "More propaganda from CNN! The people hate The Lady, and they love the SLORC. Ask anyone in the street or in the market."

Later that day in the Aung San Market—the largest in Rangoon, and named after Aung San Suu Kyi's father—and still in the company of my minder, I did ask several men, women, and a group of children. "Aung San Suu Kyi, good or bad?" One glance at my minder, Noreen, and they all understood that she would report their response. None of them answered. Whenever the people are questioned about the SLORC, the reaction is almost always the same: eyes lowered, gently shaking their heads, they pretend not to hear. Without exception, the smile that Secretary of State Albright referred to is always visible.

Occasionally, a brave soul will try and communicate. On another excursion to the Aung San market, a young man slipped a crumpled note into my hand. Later on in my room, I opened it and read in scrawled English, "SLORC kills everyone." Another time, while waiting to cross the street on Strand Road, a voice in the crowd near me shouted, "Tell the world—help us!" When I turned around, nobody would meet my gaze.

General David Abel, an affable Anglo-Burmese, is the Minister for National Planning and Economic Development. A respected economist, General Abel is responsible for evaluating every potential foreign investor or company before any venture can be approved between them and the SLORC.

A tall, slender man of nearly seventy years, General Abel resembles a bespectacled college professor. The rumor around Rangoon is that he is partly Jewish, an interesting rumor since in *The New Light of Myanmar*, the state-controlled newspaper, there have been disparaging references made concerning Aung San Suu Kyi's husband's supposed Jewish background. Curiously, he is sometimes rumored to be Indian. When I asked General Abel about his own background, however, he claimed that his father's family were German Lutherans who had come to Burma in the late nineteenth century as missionaries.

According to a Burmese national from a prestigious and old family who has known General Abel for decades, the Anglo-Burmese general prides himself on having an astute understanding of western mentality and general western business customs. As a result, General Abel is usually the one who is sent on goodwill foreign missions, and who meets with various members of western chambers of commerce and other business organizations. A man who enjoys good food and wine, General Abel has been known to boast about his "special connections" with the inner sanctums of certain foreign governments, as well as his ability to penetrate the boardrooms of many multinational corporations. One western businessman says of General Abel, "Regardless of what the deal is, or how far-fetched the scheme, David Abel will tell you it's no problem and he's the only one to get it approved by the SLORC." According to that same businessman, however, when the general fails, it usually is a spectacular and costly blunder. "I remember one deal," the man recalls, "where I was trying to sell some used hospital equipment to the SLORC from a clinic in California that had gone bankrupt. General Abel guaranteed me that the SLORC would buy it. I arranged for the stuff to be carted up and shipped to Burma where it sat in crates for months because Abel couldn't get the government to release the money. What it cost me in shipping fees was astronomical."

When I questioned General Abel about the conditions in Burma, he seemed aghast. "Rubbish, these unfounded rumors," he said. "It is the Buddhist tradition for people to volunteer to work for the betterment of the country, because we believe we get merits for the next life. It is the communists and Aung San Suu Kyi who spread rumors of forced labor, and certain writers and reporters who believe them and write lies to hurt my country. If I had a house and my house needed repair, the entire neighborhood would be there to help me and they wouldn't expect to be paid."

In its own defense, the SLORC points to the efforts it has made to clean up the pockets of squatters, claiming that it has relocated people to subsidized apartments with electricity and indoor plumbing. In the course of my travels around Rangoon, I was taken to one of those new subsidized apartments. The family who lived there was obviously expecting me as they had fruit, cold drinks, and small cakes on a table. Claiming to have been moved from a hut, they lauded the SLORC for making their lives a "paradise." What baffled me was that they all spoke perfect English and were cultured and articulate, which made me wonder if they were really a good example of a typical Burmese family who had been living in a hut. But when I asked specifically the location of the hut, and where they originally came from, what they did to earn money, they glanced at Colonel Hla Min and simply shrugged. When I pressed them, Colonel Hla Min suggested that we had a lot more to see and time was running out. And, when I asked my government guides if I could perhaps talk with other tenants in the building who had also been relocated from huts in Rangoon, the response was that Buddhist custom dictated that appointments had to be made in advance.

The SLORC also systematically denies accusations that they force entire villages and communities in the rural areas to relocate to make room for any one of the country's new international multi-million-dollar development projects. Instead, the regime claims that the only relocation it "offers" the people is to move them to better dwellings. On a subsequent trip to the border areas—without the SLORC's permission, without even a bonafide visa, since I had slipped in over the border with Thailand—I saw for myself how entire areas had been destroyed. I spoke to groups of people who had been left homeless, in fighting with Karen and other ethnic minority opposition forces or to accommodate government and international building projects.

What is certain is that the SLORC has created two distinct societies, which makes it all too easy to get the wrong impression of life for the average Burmese. The more I wandered around Rangoon accompanied by my minder, who spewed propaganda in response to my questions or comments, the more I realized how appropriate one journalist's comment had been about Burma. "Look around," the reporter said, "The country is a fascist Disneyland."

Walking around Rangoon one day, I asked my minder about the ubiquitous billboards with slogans written on them. She explained that they were there to remind the people of the SLORC's accomplishments, as well as to make sure that foreign visitors were aware of the regime's successes.

Some billboards list the SLORC's so-called social programs, such as a health care system for the poor, which, in reality, is virtually nonexistent, as is the governmentally claimed expansion of educational facilities. The most bizarre message, however, written on every billboard, regardless of the main message, was:

BEWARE OF STOOGES!

The SLORC's version of a public relations campaign would be laughable if the situation were not so tragic.

Consider that, with the exception of military hospitals, health care is so poor in Burma that the mortality rate of newborn infants is 94 per 1,000, the fourth highest in East Asia; the maternal mortality rate is the third highest in that region, with 123 deaths per 100,000 women.

Consider as well that the people are imprisoned without trial, arrested for criticizing the regime, or even for gathering in groups of more than five.

Consider that the state-owned television nightly news station shows only images of SLORC generals, resplendent in crisp uniforms with rows upon rows of gleaming medals, dedicating Buddhist temples, inspecting factories, and officiating at song-and-dance contests.

Consider that on display at the International Gem Emporium are some of the world's most precious and priceless jewels, only one example of Burma's many natural resources that are mined and polished by poverty-stricken laborers in a trade that is dominated by the military and its business associates. Curiously, despite the ridiculously low salaries of the military—including the salary of Colonel Hla Min, who claims to earn the equivalent of $50 per month—military wives all wear rare golden pearl rings or pendants, and sapphire, ruby, emerald, and diamond necklaces, bracelets, and earrings.

Consider also the SLORC's claims that several "dissidents,"

imprisoned for their pro-democracy activity at the notorious Insein Prison on the outskirts of Rangoon, died from overeating rich food, not from torture or the appalling conditions that the regime insists are more examples of vicious rumors perpetrated by the west.

* * *

Within days of my arrival in Rangoon, it wasn't necessary to ask directions to Aung San Suu Kyi's house. Although the SLORC had removed the number on the house on University Avenue to confuse people, it was a wasted effort. Everyone knows where The Lady lives.

On one of the few occasions that I found myself on my way to a meeting in Rangoon without a minder, my cab driver wondered not *if* but *when* I intended to visit The Lady, adding that the weekends are the best time, providing the police and military have not closed off her street. Having already been warned by several foreign diplomats about government spies, tapped telephones, listening devices, and hidden cameras throughout Burma, my response was instinctively cautious. Did my driver really think a visit to the street and eventually to The Lady was worth my time? After all, I had heard that the pro-democracy movement was slowly disappearing? His answer was immediate.

"The Lady is Burma," he said. "She encompasses the hopes and dreams of the people. If you don't talk to her, you will never understand the true tragedy of my country."

As the most recognizable figure of the pro-democracy movement in Burma, Daw Suu Kyi has had several incarnations in her lakeshore villa on University Avenue. As a child, she lived there with her family. As a young wife and mother living abroad in England, she returned for regular visits, accompanied by her British husband and their two sons. Finally, when she was called back to Rangoon in 1988 to care for her dying mother, the house on Inya Lake became Daw Suu Kyi's private prison when she became caught up in the violence and political unrest that erupted in August of that year.

Placed under house arrest in 1989 by the SLORC, Aung San Suu Kyi lived alone in the house for six years virtually without family or friends, her only company a radio and a maid who brought daily provisions, and an ever-present battery of armed guards who remained on duty in the garden. Released three years ago, The Lady currently lives a life of monastic simplicity, spending her days and nights working with such close colleagues as ex-General U Tin U and ex-Colonel U Kyi Maung, two former military men who began the pro-democracy movement with her in 1988, and who, along with her today, find themselves on a constant collision course with the military regime.

U Kyi Maung, one of the more visible members of the National League for Democracy, is credited with leading the NLD to victory in the 1990 elections, while U Tin U, another illustrious member of the NLD, was arrested by the SLORC at the same time as Aung San Suu Kyi. Subsequently he served six years in Insein Prison, from 1989 until 1995.

Other key members of the NLD are U Aung Shwe, who is chairman of the party, and U Lwin, who originally served as its treasurer. Along with U Aung Shwe, U Lwin was one of the original members of the Executive Committee not imprisoned after 1990, and who helped keep the movement alive. After the Executive Committee was reorganized in 1992, U Lwin was appointed Secretary.

The more SLORC has tried to diminish The Lady's presence and voice by keeping her a prisoner in her own house and by refusing even to call her by name, the more she and her now-famous villa have become the mecca for the international press and visiting foreign dignitaries. In fact, even the occasional tourist and business traveler can be counted among those who flock to 54 University Avenue, less for any interest in Burmese politics than to see for themselves the subject of so many international newspaper articles and feature stories on television and radio broadcasts throughout the world. Even more threatening

to the SLORC, however, were the crowds of Burmese, number-
ing anywhere from several hundred to several thousand, who
gathered in front of the house on any given Saturday or Sunday
afternoon—when the street wasn't barricaded and guarded by
soldiers or police—to hear The Lady speak out for a multiparty
democratic Burma. Predictably, such gatherings have since been
halted by the SLORC.

The first weekend after I arrived, several journalists told me
that it was likely that the authorities were going to allow Daw
Suu Kyi to hold her weekly meeting on that Saturday. Nothing
was certain, however, since the SLORC was unpredictable where
it concerned The Lady, often changing their mind at the last
minute for no apparent reason.

4

UNIVERSITY AVENUE is a curving tree-lined street that skirts the picturesque Inya Lake. It is the most frequently used shortcut to get from one shore to the other. Even when the street is not barricaded, truckloads of soldiers and police are stationed all over the area, hiding behind shrubs and bushes, wandering along the parameters of Inya Lake, and stationed in intervals along adjoining roads.

On that particular Saturday afternoon, seated in the backseat of a colleague's car as we headed toward 54 University Avenue, I somehow couldn't shake the feeling that we were being followed. Getting out of the car in front of the house, I proceeded to the gate but was stopped by a man dressed in civilian clothes who asked me to produce my passport and to provide the name of the hotel where I was staying in Rangoon. After complying with his request, he waved me on. Apparently, my name was not on his list of undesirables that day, which meant that I wasn't asked to leave the area, or, worse, to leave the country.

It was early Saturday morning when we arrived, and in anticipation of the event, people had already begun gathering in front of Daw Suu Kyi's house, sitting cross-legged on the ground or milling around near the entrance to the gate. Some of the audience were young—office workers, lawyers, physicians, academics—while others were elderly, white-haired and bone-thin, their

teeth stained yellow from years of chewing betel nuts, their with-
ered bodies wrapped in *longyis*. Monks mingled with laborers,
nuns with students, while vendors weaved through the crowd
hawking bottled water and grilled chicken, and stray skeletal
dogs picked at the scraps.

Toward late morning, several of Daw Suu Kyi's supporters
dragged two loudspeakers down the driveway to the edge of the
road where they hoisted them into a tree, attaching the wires to
an amplifier. What fascinated me even more than the excitement
of the people or the preparations of her staff, were the government informers who mingled with the crowd. As I stood around,
taking notes in cryptic shorthand, several young Burmese men,
sunglasses covering their eyes, edged up to me, peering over my
shoulder to see what I was writing.

The exterior of The Lady's house is in disrepair, with paint
flaking from the villa's walls. The interior is in equally dismal
disrepair, with large spots of black mold creeping up the stucco
walls and ceilings toward a clump of damp rot only inches away
from a long fluorescent light fixture. The rooms are mostly bare,
and whatever furniture had not been sold off by Aung San Suu
Kyi to buy food when she was under house arrest is old and
worn. Even the piano, once a treasured family heirloom, sits un-
tuned, unplayed, and dusty in the living room.

Although Aung San Suu Kyi has become visible only since
1988 when there was widespread and violent opposition to the
regime, her supporters insist that throughout the two decades
and more that she lived outside Burma, she kept a close watch
on political events. Many members of the NLD, and other political colleagues, as well as human-rights advocates throughout
the world, have created a set of retroactive political positions and
aspirations said to be held by Daw Suu Kyi, to prove that she was
committed to the pro-democracy movement even before it actually existed.

The party line coming out of the exile NLD headquarters in
Washington, and echoed by a variety of pro-democracy and
human-rights activists, is that when Daw Suu Kyi returned to

Rangoon in 1988 to care for her ailing mother, she was already very much aware that her destiny was to finish the job that her father had begun before he was assassinated on the eve of Burma's independence. Yet, when asked, Daw Suu Kyi herself readily admits that she had no political aspirations when she first arrived in Rangoon. "When I arrived in Rangoon to take care of my mother," she explains, "my only intention regarding politics was to start several libraries in my father's memory."

There are others who knew Daw Suu Kyi throughout her college days in England who claim that during all those years abroad, she never involved herself with any Burmese exile groups, or read Burmese newspapers to keep abreast of the political situation. According to those same people, other than several trips every few years to visit her family in Rangoon, Daw Suu Kyi remained far from the country of her birth.

Her detractors go even further, however, when they insist that she was transformed into a typical western woman as a result of attending school in India and England, working at the United Nations in New York, and eventually marrying a British subject and embracing the culture and customs of his world. During a meeting in Rangoon with General Khin Nyunt, the most visible face of the SLORC, he tried to explain to me the regime's view of her.

"Aung San Suu Kyi did not lead a normal life in accordance with our religious teachings and customs and traditions," General Khin Nyunt told me. "Unfortunately, she is not leading the life of a normal citizen today because she is trying to cause political confusion and instability and unrest when we finally have peace and tranquility in the country. Although we love and respect her father, it is very difficult for us to have the same feelings for her because of her actions. Frankly, if Aung San Suu Kyi had come back and worked for the country and married a Myanmar citizen, she might have been able to become a national leader."

According to Colonel Hla Min, my main contact with the SLORC, "The Lady was the daughter of a Burmese national hero who made her life on another continent." He adds, "And, when she did return to lay a wreath on her father's grave, her presence evoked neither nostalgia nor hope in the people as she guarded her privacy and limited her visits to immediate family."

In fact, the SLORC takes the position that had the Burmese Army not insisted that Aung San Suu Kyi return to Rangoon to care for the widow of their national hero, she never would have appeared during a time of violent crisis. As if to imply that Aung San Suu Kyi not only forgot about her country, but neglected her mother as well, General Khin Nyunt told me, "When Aung San Suu Kyi came back in 1988, it was at our invitation and insistence that she care for her ailing mother."

Although urban disturbances in 1988 were not all based on the people's desire for multiparty democracy, there are many people in Burma and throughout the world who credit Aung San Suu Kyi for harnessing the political unrest and uniting the people toward a common goal of democracy that ultimately garnered international support. George Soros, the Hungarian-born philanthropist, is one. Soros is the founder of the Open Society Institute, which promotes freedom and democracy throughout the world, as well as the founder and main financial backer of The Burma Project, a think tank whose goals are to increase international awareness of Burma's problems and potential, and to help Burma make a transition into a free, open, and just society. The Hungarian billionaire says of Aung San Suu Kyi, "She is the only reason why the world has become aware of the SLORC's practice of torture, summary and arbitrary executions, forced labor, including forced portering for the military, and abuse of women, among a litany of other offenses that it also commits against its own citizens."

Contradictory opinions also exist concerning Daw Suu Kyi's political ability to speak for the Burmese, even among those people who share her aspirations for the country. For instance, several prominent members of the NLD, her own pro-democracy party, believe that the only reason The Lady has achieved international acclaim is that her stand for freedom and human-rights unarguably speaks for itself, especially in a country that has long been famous for its repressive regimes and military juntas. Yet there are others, who oppose the SLORC and who have spent arduous years in prison for their opposition, who insist that although The Lady is popular with the international community, she does not have a solid base of support within the country. One prominent dissident who lives in Rangoon says, "Some of the urban city dwellers are sympathetic to her because they are more sophisticated and have access to media reports on Suu Kyi, while people outside Rangoon are not very interested in her at all. For these people, their biggest concern is whether they have enough to eat, or whether the army will come and take their homes, or force them to work as porters. They have not yet made the connection between the brutality of the regime and Suu Kyi's promises to make their lives better."

Even the SLORC has conflicting opinions concerning The Lady. When the regime is in a collectively benevolent mood toward her, they claim that it is only her charm, beauty, and command of English that make her the most sought-after soundbite for countless media reports and human-rights groups. Professor Khin Maung Nyunt, the Oxford-educated Deputy Minister of Education, endorses that opinion when he says, "The Lady is loved by the West because of her command of the English language, which is naturally good because she married an Englishman and has lived all her life in the U.K. But why should my government be blamed for not speaking English since it is not our mother tongue?"

When the SLORC is more malevolently disposed, they insist that Daw Suu Kyi is nothing more than a tool for the communists. Often, they refer to her as a "western fashion girl" or "political stunt princess" or, more savagely, as an "ax handle of the neo-colonialists."

Colonel Hla Min preferred to focus on Daw Suu Kyi's alleged communist connections when he told me, "The Communist Party cells saw her as a great advantage because she is the daughter of our national hero. They believed that if they could push her into the front and take advantage of her position, it would serve their purposes."

Many analysts, however, consider such statements part of the propaganda war. One Burmese-watcher commented, "The SLORC has called Suu Kyi just about everything, including a communist. In 1989, when world communism collapsed and the Communist Party in Burma along with it, the SLORC began calling Suu Kyi a neo-imperialist."

When it comes to Aung San Suu Kyi, rumors are not limited to the SLORC, or to her political ambitions. Several journalists who have visited the house and interviewed Daw Suu Kyi later claimed that there are no family photographs or other personal memorabilia on display. As a result, many of those same journalists maintain that Daw Suu Kyi has apparently forgotten her family somewhere along the way, and instead devotes herself entirely to the cause of freedom for her people. Barbara Bradley, a journalist for the *Christian Science Monitor,* is one such reporter.

In an article she wrote on Daw Suu Kyi that appeared in *Vogue* magazine, Bradley wondered how the pro-democracy leader could leave her two small children and husband indefinitely to take up a cause, however noble, thousands of miles away. After interviewing Daw Suu Kyi at her lakeside home, Bradley wrote:

". . . I survey the room, crammed with artifacts from her political life. We sit at the scuffed teak table that was used for strategy sessions . . . and has once again become the nerve center of democratic activities. Pinned to the wall behind her hangs a huge textile stencil of her father. . . . Gracing another wall are old sepia photographs of her parents but none of her husband and sons. It is a political museum and points to where her future lies."

Contrary to those reports, the second floor of the house—strictly off-limits to anyone except close friends and immediate family—is filled with personal touches and mementos. If photographs of her famous father and other international figures adorn the walls downstairs, they have been left exactly as Aung San Suu Kyi's mother arranged them when she occupied the house. Now that Daw Suu Kyi lives there, photographs of her British husband, Michael Aris, and their two sons, Alexander and Kim, are in the upstairs portion. In Suu's private quarters as well, there are sepia-colored photographs of her mother and brothers, along with more intimate poses of her father with friends and colleagues, all of whom fought for Burmese independence from the British so many decades before.

Included among Suu's treasured possessions are books and letters written by friends and other literary works that she reads voraciously in her spare time, as well as reminders of her school days in India and England when she was a teenager and later on, as a university student. Although the bedroom where Daw Suu Kyi sleeps is furnished sparsely, there are the basic necessities, including a mosquito net over the bed, and even what she considers to be several luxuries, such as blankets that have been in her family since she was a child, including one Japanese spread that covered her parents' bridal bed.

Once an avid cook, The Lady now has little time to experiment with complicated dishes or even to prepare simple daily meals, and the kitchen bears witness to that fact. The refrigerator is meagerly stocked, the cupboards contain the minimum of provisions, and the counters and table are often strewn with papers and documents pertaining to her work.

Shortly before the speech was scheduled to begin on that Saturday, I watched as a desk was placed precariously on top of the gate. Within minutes, Daw Suu Kyi appeared from behind the shrubs and flowers to be helped up on top of the desk where she stood and where she was greeted by cheers and applause that continued throughout her talk.

I had brought along a student from Yangon University to translate Daw Suu Kyi's speech into English for me, and as he did, it struck me that The Lady's manner and choice of words were somehow reminiscent of the character Chauncey Gardner in Jerzy Kosinski's book *Being There*. Similar to the pronouncements of the honest and naive Gardner, whatever Daw Suu Kyi said that day, however simple, was met by outright euphoria by her listeners. For example, in one instance she cautioned the people, "Think before you act; avoid having extreme ideas." The reaction was cheers and whistles. When I asked a man standing next to me what exactly she had meant by that particular message, his response was immediate. Shrugging, he confessed that he wasn't sure, although it didn't matter since the people were so entranced with Suu Kyi's beauty, and poetic command of the Burmese language, that the substance of what she said was less important than the fact of her just being there.

There is no doubt that as a public speaker, Aung San Suu Kyi is poised and gifted. As a public figure, she is dedicated to the concept of bringing democracy to Burma, and deeply believes in her moral obligation to achieve that goal. As the symbol of the pro-democracy movement, there is no one better than she to have brought the abhorrent conditions in Burma to the attention of the international community.

The general format of the Saturday and Sunday meetings is that Daw Suu Kyi answers questions that the audience has submitted in writing in advance, topics ranging from advice on food or health to her opinions on politics or literature. Often, she speaks several words of English for the benefit of any foreigners who happen to be in the audience, and who respond with the same level of enthusiasm as the Burmese. What is most touching about Daw Suu Kyi's special relationship with the crowd, however, is that at the end of her talks, she never fails to instruct everybody to return home quickly. There is always the threat that government spies, police, or soldiers will suddenly arrest random civilians, or in extreme cases, open fire into the crowd. Perched on top of the desk, Daw Suu Kyi surveys the people as they disperse, making sure that everyone departs without arrest or harassment.

At the end of the gathering that day, I was able to speak with several Burmese, all of whom insisted that they admired Suu Kyi less as a political figure than as a much-loved heroine who allows them to forget the harsh realities of life under the SLORC—if only for several hours. Regardless of whom I questioned that day, the answer was that The Lady was admired as a symbol of their dreams and aspirations. A construction worker in the crowd said simply, "Whatever happens, she gives us hope."

General U Tin U, one of Daw Suu Kyi's close colleagues, joined the Burmese Army in 1943 when he was only sixteen years old. After World War II ended, he was one of the 150 Burmese officers who was given a commission in the reorganized Burmese Army that was founded by General Aung San right before the country gained its independence from the British. For him, the slender figure with the beautiful face reminiscent of an ivory carving with her huge dark liquid eyes evokes memories of another era. "I knew her father," General U Tin U recalls, "and she reminds me of him, the way she smiles and tilts her head. All her gestures are similar to his, even the way she speaks in short, concise sentences."

There are other members of the NLD, however, who express concern that her relationship with the Burmese people is not unlike a love affair when the partners are in the first blush of romance and passion. The danger, they explain, is that the excitement will eventually fade and the lovers will grow apart if there is nothing substantial to replace the newness of the affair.

By contrast, many observers see Daw Suu Kyi on a larger international stage. Said one western specialist, "When Suu Kyi talks about human-rights and democracy, people find it understandable and interesting because Burma's problems are universal. Regardless of the substance in her talks, or concrete programs for democracy, she is taken seriously because many people believe she represents their only hope for a better life."

A young Burmese lawyer who is a faithful member of the audience every time Daw Suu Kyi is allowed to speak says, "We may never get democracy, but the people will always love Suu Kyi. She has already sacrificed so much for us."

5

For the majority of the Burmese people, the most important sacrifice that Aung San Suu Kyi made for them was not giving in to the SLORC's demands during the six years that the military kept her under house arrest. The SLORC insists that at any time during those years, The Lady always had the choice of safe passage out of Burma in a chauffeur-driven car to the airport and a free one-way ticket back to England where she had been living for the last two decades. For Daw Suu Kyi, that was always an unacceptable alternative. It is to her credit that she refused, a sign of courage and stamina that she remained steadfast in her commitment to bring democracy to her country of birth.

Since Daw Suu Kyi's release, the SLORC continues to close University Avenue sporadically and without warning, usually for hours or sometimes even for days, forcing traffic and pedestrians to take the long way around, and even obliging residents to prove that they live there before they are allowed to enter. For local merchants and cab drivers, betting on whether the street is open or closed has become an amusing pastime, one more example of how the Burmese respond to a series of occupiers and oppressors with their usual good humor.

During the three years since Aung San Suu Kyi has been officially released from house arrest, the SLORC has intensified its control over all Burmese citizens, as well as on journalists and tourists. When foreign diplomats are the target of government informers, those diplomats usually escape without violent consequences. Even with Aung San Suu Kyi, the SLORC is unable to act with impunity because of her high international profile. It is quite another story when it comes to the majority of Burmese citizens. Life for them has not only gotten more difficult, but punishments for infringements of SLORC-imposed laws have become more harsh.

"One of the saddest things about Burma," Daw Suu Kyi maintains, "is that there is a climate of suspicion that makes everybody fearful that someone is an informer. To build up a climate of trust is going to be one of the most difficult jobs."

Hospitality among the Burmese people, for example, once a national treasure, now has dire consequences. No longer can friends and family arrive unannounced at anyone's home, bearing food and gifts and simply looking forward to a pleasurable visit. Even newly married couples who, for financial reasons, have no home of their own, are not allowed to spend a night together without official registration.

Under the SLORC, all Burmese must report their movements by filling out a "guest list" for the local authorities before nine o'clock each evening if they intend to visit or sleep away from home or if they intend to receive visitors. Officially, the form is known as "Government Form 10." It is not unusual for soldiers to institute random checks in the middle of the night, counting heads to make sure that the number of people in any given house corresponds with the total number of residents listed on Form 10. Disobeying this rule results in fines or imprisonment for both guest and host.

Recently, the SLORC has made it even more difficult for visiting dignitaries, especially various human-rights groups and representatives from the United Nations and the Red Cross, to obtain visas to enter Burma. According to Michael Aris, he has been refused a visa to visit his wife since July 1995. Kim and Alexander, Daw Suu Kyi's sons, have been allowed to visit her more frequently. In fact, in September 1997, one of her sons spent time with her in Rangoon.

When asked the reasons for these measures, the SLORC offers a variety of excuses. For instance, Form 10, according to the SLORC, is nothing more than a bureaucratic error. "During General Ne Win's regime when there were food rations," Colonel Hla Min explained, "Form 10 was the only way to keep track of who lived where in order to supply sufficient food." According to official word from the SLORC, Form 10 will be discontinued "any day now."

As far as prohibiting visitors, or more specifically, human-rights groups—or even Daw Suu Kyi's family—the SLORC claims that these visitors are less interested in the conditions of life in Burma than they are in creating problems for the SLORC. "All they're interested in is spewing propaganda for The Lady," Colonel Hla Min stated.

What about The Lady's husband and children? "Why should we do anything to make life pleasant for The Lady?" Colonel Hla Min asked.

In response to why University Avenue is often closed, and Daw Suu Kyi is forced to remain inside her compound, the SLORC claims that they contain The Lady for her own protection, to ensure her safety in an atmosphere that has allegedly become increasingly hostile toward her and her party's efforts to promote freedom and democracy.

Several months after I left Rangoon, in the spring of 1996, the car in which Aung San Suu Kyi was riding was stoned by a group of Burmese. The SLORC immediately announced that The Lady was the target of aggression by the people who are increasingly in favor of the regime. The truth is that almost all acts of hostility against Daw Suu Kyi are government-inspired.

Several months before Daw Suu Kyi was released from house arrest, the SLORC created a pro-government movement called the Union Solidarity and Development Association, or USDA, which is made up of students and ordinary civilians who are recruited, threatened, or paid to join, and who are coerced into showing up for rallies and demonstrations in favor of the military regime. In her recent book, *Letters from Burma*, Daw Suu Kyi wrote, "Often members of the USDA are collected from various townships and told to beat up members of the NLD...."

According to several other foreign diplomats, the SLORC's goal when they created the USDA was to promote the idea in the media that the SLORC was gaining popularity and more support than the NLD.

More recently, in June 1996, the government began staging dozens of protests across the country where thousands of people shouted slogans and made speeches denouncing the democracy movement. In response, Aung San Suu Kyi warned a crowd of supporters gathered in front of her house to refuse to go to any government-staged rallies that denounced the prodemocracy movement. "Be aware that those rallies are not a real sign of support for the ruling military."

Her warnings, however, can and often do produce dire consequences.

When any Burmese refuses to join the USDA or participate in mass demonstrations of support for the regime, the penalties range from heavy monetary fines to denying students admission to university, preventing them from taking their exams, confiscation of personal property, and, in some cases, jail.

Another reason the SLORC often gives for preventing Aung San Suu Kyi from leaving her house is that she has become a national nuisance who disrupts the "stability, peace, prosperity, and law and order" that they (the SLORC) have achieved throughout the country.

Logic refutes all the SLORC's excuses.

If the SLORC had truly achieved stability, peace, prosperity, and law and order throughout the country, political meetings between Daw Suu Kyi and the press or visiting colleagues, or even simple social visits between friends and family, would certainly not threaten what the regime has allegedly accomplished.

The reality is that despite their tactics of terror, the SLORC's hold over the people is so tenuous and weak that they are afraid to allow any liberties that might result in an organized effort to overthrow the regime.

One of the questions that plagued me during my trip to Burma was why the SLORC released Daw Suu Kyi if they continue to deny her and her colleagues freedom of movement. Curiously, both sides of the struggle offered the same explanation: not only was there enormous international pressure and financial incentive to release Daw Suu Kyi, but the military also believed that they had the appropriate force to counter any pro-Suu Kyi or pro-democracy demonstrations.

Douglas Rasmussen, the Counselor at the United States Embassy in Rangoon, says, "At the time of Suu Kyi's release, the SLORC thought it was dealing from a position of strength not only because of the USDA, but also because foreign investment was pouring into Burma. And, don't forget, the SLORC had also managed at that time to avoid sanctions or boycotts from either the United States or the European Union. The problem was that, as usual, the regime miscalculated the power and popularity of The Lady."

The struggle between the military regime and the pro-democracy movement is not only a violent conflict between civilians and soldiers, but also a war of wills between a group of intractable military men and one stubbornly idealistic woman. To ensure their own survival, the SLORC is obliged constantly to minimize Daw Suu Kyi's popularity with the Burmese people.

General Maung Maung, during our first meeting, interpreted Aung San Suu Kyi's impact on the Burmese during the weekly meetings that she holds—when allowed—in front of her house this way: "Yangon has something like 4.6 million people. If you have 4 or 5 thousand who turn out to hear The Lady, it is less than 1 percent of the total population. You see, if the students really supported her, there would be more than 17 thousand from the university alone. Frankly, if you have a cockfight, the same number of people will turn up."

Colonel Hla Min went even further when he posed the following rhetorical question. "Who are the people who come to hear The Lady speak?" he wondered. "Sometimes I pass by and they look like quite a rough crowd. In fact, I am told they are paid to come. Last Saturday I went to a monastery to give rice and in the crowd I saw an ex-politician who lives nearby. He told me that in 1988 when there were anti-government demonstrations, he used to give out *kyats* to people so they would go out and demonstrate, something like Rent-A-Crowd. If things were genuine, the students would be at these Saturday talks, but The Lady refuses to realize this and never will unless she comes to her gate one day and finds it deserted, which is what I predict will happen. People will eventually get bored."

Yet, even among SLORC officials there is disagreement concerning The Lady's political longevity. Professor Khin Maung Nyunt, during a meeting with me at the University of Yangon, disagreed with Colonel Hla Min's assessment. "She is a hot-headed person," the professor claimed. "She will never go away quietly."

Since 1988, when Aung San Suu Kyi first became visibly involved in the struggle for democracy, the people have become even more devoted and loyal to her, more committed to the cause of freedom in Burma, and more dependent on her to bring their plight to the world's attention. If that were not the case, the NLD would have never survived—and grown—despite all the obstacles the government has put in its way since 1988.

But while most of Daw Suu Kyi's supporters and colleagues dismiss the SLORC's notion that the people will eventually get bored, they do perceive another very real danger.

During Aung San Suu Kyi's weekly talks, or included in her interviews that constantly appear in the foreign press, she often sends the potentially dangerous message that "courage comes from cultivating the habit of refusing to let fear dictate one's actions." It is a philosophy that she cherishes, and one that was the inspiration for the title of her first book, *Freedom from Fear*. In any other atmosphere, Suu Kyi's words might have only a positive effect. In Burma, those words are dangerous.

One of the most difficult challenges that Aung San Suu Kyi

faces is not only to bring democracy to Burma, but to achieve that goal without putting the people at risk. It is a difficult task since the Burmese people have been shut off from the rest of the world for decades, and do not believe democracy and freedom to be their inalienable rights. As a result, Daw Suu Kyi's role lies somewhere between that of a politician who leads the people toward democracy, and a spiritual figure who encourages people to take their own initiatives in ridding the country of an oppressive regime.

U Bo Hla Tint, the Finance Minister of the National Coalition Government of the Union of Burma, consisting of a dozen NLD MPs who have their exile headquarters in Washington, D.C., explains, "Suu Kyi tells the Burmese people that they must act for themselves and not only look to her to save them. Actually, the reality is that the people are unable to do what they need to do because they were isolated for nearly three decades, which makes them unable to understand what their human-rights are, and what freedom and democracy are. How do you teach them?"

It is a difficult question to answer.

6

AUNG SAN SUU KYI was two years old when her father was
assassinated in 1948. She has said that her father died when
she was too young to remember him. "But even though I never
really knew him," she adds, "I was always told how much the
Burmese people loved and revered him."

Learning about her father would become almost an obses-
sion. The desire to understand not only her father's feelings, but
also his philosophy and commitment to the cause of independence, would eventually translate into Suu Kyi's own pledge to
finish the job that her father had begun.

There are people who claim that Aung San Suu Kyi's political
destiny began when she was born; others maintain that it began
in 1988 when she arrived in Rangoon to care for her mother.
While destiny is an abstraction, there is little doubt that Daw
Suu Kyi's presence in Burma during a time of protest and rebellion rekindled the image of General Aung San in the hearts and
minds of the Burmese people. Despite Aung San Suu Kyi's illustrious name and legacy and her ability to grasp the country's
complicated political situation, when she arrived in Burma in
1988, she was still somewhat of a mystery to the majority of
Burmese people. To understand Daw Suu Kyi, it's important to
understand the three major losses that she suffered and that
profoundly influenced her.

By her own admission, the first trauma in her life that affected her deeply was the death of her father. "Because he died so young, it's difficult for me to think of him as an old person. I tend to look upon him as a friend as well as a father. I feel as if he is somebody who would have stood by me when I was in trouble. I always think, 'I may be alone, but I know I have your backing.'"

The second tragedy was the death of her brother. "In some ways," Suu Kyi admits, "I believe my brother's death affected me more than my father's. I was seven-and-a-half when he died and we were very close. We shared the same room and played together."

The incident happened in the spring of 1956, on the shores of Inya Lake. The little boy had dropped his toy gun and went back to retrieve it when his sandal came off in the mud. Running to his sister, he handed her the toy gun before racing back to get his shoe. He never returned. Apparently, the child was swept up in the mud and waters of the lake.

The third event was the loss of her country when General Ne Win launched his coup in 1962 and took power away from U Nu, the democratically elected Prime Minister. Daw Suu Kyi was only fifteen when she accompanied her mother, Daw Khin Kyi, who had been appointed Burmese ambassador to India. Remaining there until 1964, Daw Suu Kyi would not return to Burma on a permanent basis until 1988.

During the first few years of Ne Win's regime, when Daw Suu Kyi lived in India, she explored the lessons of passive resistance of Mahatma Ghandi and Jawaharlal Nehru. Her education and background gave her the opportunity to be well-versed in several different cultures. Although Daw Suu Kyi was raised as a Buddhist, her maternal grandfather had been a converted Christian. Often, when she was a child, he would ask her to read to him from the New Testament.

Upon arriving in India, Daw Suu Kyi spent one year in a strict convent school where, in addition to her academic studies, she learned flower arrangement, horseback riding, piano, cooking, sewing, and Japanese. The following year she attended Delhi University, where she read political science. Patricia Gore-Booth, whose husband, Sir Paul, later Lord Paul, was Britain's High Commissioner in New Delhi while Daw Khin Kyi was the Burmese ambassador, became a close friend. When Daw Suu Kyi was accepted at St. Hugh's College at Oxford, she left Delhi University. It was then that Lady Gore-Booth suggested to Daw Khin Kyi that her daughter make their London home her base. At the Gore-Booth house in Chelsea, Daw Suu Kyi not only met interesting and powerful politicians and intellectuals, but she also made friends with the group of young people who knew the Gore-Booth's twin sons. Included among them were another set of twins, Michael and Anthony Aris. Tall, handsome, rugged, and brilliant young men, the Aris twins were both studying to be Orientalists.

Lady Gore-Booth recalls that for Michael Aris, it was love at first sight when he met the beautiful Burmese girl. From the very beginning, however, Daw Suu Kyi announced that she had no intention of ever marrying anyone other than a Burmese.

During an interview with Anthony Aris and his French wife, Marie-Laure, he insisted that "from the very beginning of their courtship, we all knew that some day Suu would return to her country. It was just something that Michael lived with and we all accepted as a foregone conclusion."

As an undergraduate at St. Hugh's in Oxford, Daw Suu Kyi was remembered as very demure and genuinely innocent, yet with a strong sense of belonging to the Burmese elite. Ann Pasternak Slater, who met Suu Kyi at St. Hugh's College in 1964, is quoted in *Freedom from Fear*, "Suu's tight trim *longyi* (the Burmese version of the sarong) and upright carriage, her firm moral convictions and inherited social grace, contrasted sharply with the tatty dress and careless manner, vague liberalism, and uncertain sexual morality of my English contemporaries." According to Slater, although the two women were and still are close, most of Suu's friends during those college years were Indian and African, one of many indications that Daw Suu Kyi was determined not to limit herself to English friends in a homogenized British atmosphere. Slater recalls, "Even with familiarity, much remained exotic about Suu, her proud parentage, above all."

Two years after Daw Suu Kyi received her degree, after a brief stint at teaching and another conducting research with the historian Hugh Tinker, she left for New York, where she stayed with another family friend, Ma Than E.

As a Burmese national living in England in 1947, Ma Than E had first met Daw Suu Kyi's father when General Aung San traveled to London with a Burmese delegation to meet with British Labour Prime Minister Clement Attlee. In fact, it was in London in January 1947 that Prime Minister Attlee and General Aung San signed an agreement calling for full Burmese independence.

Ma Than E recalls how, on many evenings when General Aung San had no other appointments, she would be invited to dine with him and the entire Burmese delegation in their suite at the Dorchester Hotel. "After the meal, crowding in front of a rather feebly glowing electric fire," Ma Than E reminisces, "there would be talk of pre-war times, the days of their military training in Japan, and the days of hope to come."

Ma Than E had spent most of the war years in India and later in New Delhi, working for All Radio India, which broadcast throughout the Far East in many different languages, and which reached Japanese-occupied territories throughout Asia. Later, she went to San Francisco on the same broadcasting assignment for the Voice of America, at that time called the U.S. Office of War Information.

When Daw Suu Kyi arrived in New York to stay with Ma Than E, the older woman had just started working at United Nations headquarters, having recently returned from four years in Algeria. The initial plan was that Daw Suu Kyi would study with Frank Trager, a professor of International Affairs at New York University, where she planned to do postgraduate studies. Trager had spent several years in Burma and had a broad-ranging interest in Southeast Asia. Although he was very interested in having the young Burmese woman as a student, and was encouraging of her work, he began to see how difficult it was for her to travel every day on the bus from Ma Than E's apartment near the United Nations to New York University's Washington Square campus in Greenwich Village. At Ma Than E's suggestion, Daw Suu Kyi decided to resume her studies at a later date and instead apply for a job at the United Nations, which was only a five-minute walk from the apartment.

After a series of applications, interviews, and recommendations, Daw Suu Kyi was finally hired as part of a select staff that monitored the deliberations and activities of the Advisory Committee on Administrative and Budgetary Questions. Members of this committee were chosen not as representatives of their respective countries, but rather for their expertise on financial matters. The fundamental responsibility of the committee was to appraise, comment on, modify, and approve the budgets for all the specialized agencies of the United Nations, including the World Health Organization. Daw Suu Kyi remained on the committee for more than three years at the United Nations during the same period that U Thant, a fellow countryman, was Secretary General.

While Daw Suu Kyi was in New York, she corresponded with Michael Aris. In fact, after Daw Suu Kyi was placed under house arrest by the SLORC, Michael made portions of that correspondence public in an effort to raise money during the six years of his wife's detention. Many supporters and colleagues claim that the letters prove that even then Daw Suu Kyi had not been merely thrown into the middle of an uprising in 1988, but rather had always known that her destiny would one day be to play a role in Burmese politics.

"I only ask one thing," Suu wrote in one letter, "that should my people need me, you would help me to do my duty by them." In another, "Would you mind very much should such a situation arise? How probable it is I do not know, but the possibility is there." And in yet another, "I am beset by fears that circumstances and national considerations might tear us apart just when we are so happy in each other that separation would be a torment. And yet such fears are futile and inconsequential if we love and cherish each other as much as we can while we can. I am sure love and compassion will triumph in the end."

What happened next in Suu's life could be attributed only to that moment in any woman's life when she realizes that she is in love. As she found herself missing Michael more and more, she realized that a career at the United Nations, however prestigious, would never be as satisfying as becoming his wife and the mother of his children. When Suu came to that decision, however, Michael was thousands of miles away, working in Bhutan as a tutor to the royal family and acting as official translator to the Bhutan government.

In 1971, Daw Suu Kyi left for Burma on home leave. Stopping in India to visit friends, she continued on to Bhutan to see Michael. It was during that visit that the couple decided to marry.

On January 1, 1972, Aung San Suu Kyi married Michael Aris in a Buddhist ceremony at the Chelsea home of her surrogate parents, Lord and Lady Gore-Booth. Shortly after that, the couple returned to Bhutan.

By then, Suu had already resigned her position at the United Nations, and Bhutan had just become a member. By a stroke of luck and because of her experience in New York, Daw Suu Kyi was hired by the Foreign Minister of Bhutan to advise him on all matters concerning the United Nations. For a little less than a year, the Foreign Minister had the benefit of Daw Suu Kyi's experience to explain United Nations' procedures and protocol—until Daw Suu Kyi and Michael returned to England, where he would enter into a doctoral program at London University. Shortly after that, Michael began his academic career at Oxford. Their first son, Alexander, was born in 1973, and a second son, Kim, arrived in 1977.

For the first few years of their marriage, Daw Suu Kyi was busy with Alexander and engrossed in her own studies in English literature, while Michael was getting his graduate degree in Tibetan studies. By her own admission, Daw Suu Kyi had little involvement with the Burmese émigré community in London, or with the anti–Ne Win movement that was gathering momentum.

It wasn't until 1977, however, after the birth of Kim, that several events occurred that would influence her life. In 1977, a Buddhist monk, Rewata Dhamma, who had known Daw Suu Kyi and her mother when they were in India, came to visit. Apparently, Suu had seen the monk at the Buddhist center at Oxford where she had come with her husband and two sons, in the company of several Tibetan lamas. Approaching him, Suu introduced her family, and asked if he would be willing to teach her sons about Buddhism. He agreed. During the course of their visits together, Daw Suu Kyi told Rewata Dhamma that she was also studying Burmese language, culture, politics, history, and tradition. Years later, the Buddhist monk would say that at the time he had the distinct impression that Daw Suu Kyi was preparing herself in the event her country needed her.

The real turning point in Daw Suu Kyi's life occurred also in 1977, which was the year she celebrated her thirty-second birthday—the age her father had been when he was assassinated. From that moment on, those close to Suu claim that there was almost a mystical awareness of her loss. It is not difficult to imagine how Daw Suu Kyi suddenly perceived time in an entirely different context, time that would become increasingly out of sync with what had once been a natural earthly order. From the day that she turned thirty-two, Aung San Suu Kyi would forever be older than her father, while General Aung San would forever be younger than his child.

As if possessed by an insatiable thirst to learn as much as possible about the father whom she had barely known, Suu decided to research her father's life. Already able to speak Japanese, she took advanced courses to understand better and to read all relevant documents that covered that period of time. According to Michael Aris, Daw Suu Kyi's goal was to write a biography of her father.

In 1985, accompanied by her younger son, Kim, Daw Suu Kyi accepted a fellowship at Kyoto University in Japan, where she intended to research her father's life, especially as it concerned his activities with the Japanese during the war.

Interestingly, Maureen Aung-Thwin, a friend during her days in Kyoto, and the current (1997) director of the The Burma Project in New York, funded by George Soros, recalls that Suu rarely mentioned her husband during that year. "It was as if she didn't have a husband," Maureen says. "She never once said anything about missing him . . . and actually, it seemed that the farther she was from him, the better it was for her, or at least more convenient for what she wanted to do with her life."

Perhaps what Maureen Aung-Thwin instinctively felt was that during that time in Japan, Daw Suu Kyi became aware that she would be forced to make a choice between family and country. "Once, Suu asked my opinion very indirectly," Maureen recalls. "She wanted to know if it was right for her to choose her country over her children. Of course, I said that I would choose my family." According to Maureen, Suu replied that it was a dilemma for her. In the end, Maureen contends, it was obvious that her conclusion was to choose her country.

It is not clear whether Daw Suu Kyi ever made a conscious decision to choose country over family. When she returned to Burma in 1988, it was to care for her mother. Later on, when she was placed under house arrest by the SLORC, which had assumed power in 1988 after pro-democracy protests had caused the collapse of the former socialist government, she was forced to make a choice: to stay and oppose the regime or return to her family.

From the beginning of Daw Suu Kyi's detention, the SLORC constantly stated that The Lady was free to leave the country at any time. In response, Aung San Suu Kyi consistently rejected the conditions, vowing that she would never compromise her ambitions to bring democracy to Burma. In fact, at one point she sent the following message to the SLORC. "You will have to take me to the airport in chains," she said, "because otherwise I will never leave."

Michael Aung-Thwin, Maureen's brother and a Burmese

scholar, also knew Daw Suu Kyi when she studied in Japan. According to Michael, Suu considered herself part of the Burmese aristocracy, someone who carried with her "a self-fulfilling sense of entitlement to the throne of power that her father had vacated."

"She was charming, intelligent, and very stubborn," Michael Aung-Thwin recalls. "She was her father's daughter and often expressed her role as guardian of his honor and memory in very authoritarian ways."

According to Aung-Thwin, she once told him, with a twinkle in her eye, "It is my destiny to rule Burma." Yet, when he pointed out that having a famous name was certain to make her ascent to power that much easier, she balked at the notion of using her father's name to further her own political aspirations. "I will do it myself," Daw Suu Kyi answered. And, in a curious way, she did.

While it was a combination of factors that changed the destiny of Burma, it was a personal tragedy that took Daw Suu Kyi away from a life of quiet domesticity in England and into the middle of violent civil unrest half a world away.

7

IN MARCH 1988 Aung San Suu Kyi was living in Oxford, England, with her husband and their sons, then aged fifteen and twelve. Along with bringing up her family and entertaining a constant stream of visitors who stayed for an evening or for a month, Suu Kyi had just resumed her academic career at the School of Oriental and African Studies at London University.

When the telephone rang on the evening of March 31, Suu Kyi and her husband were alone, reading and studying, their sons tucked away in bed. Years later, Michael would write that from the moment his wife put down the phone that night, he somehow knew that their lives would never be the same.

The call was from a close family friend in Rangoon, informing Suu Kyi that her mother had suffered a severe stroke. Almost immediately, Suu Kyi began packing. The next morning she was on a plane for Burma.

When Aung San Suu Kyi arrived in Rangoon to care for her mother, General Ne Win's military socialist government had been in power for twenty-six years, during which time Burma had gone from being one of the richest nations in Southeast Asia to one of the poorest, most isolated, and most corrupt countries in the world.

In August 1987, with the economy plunging to the lowest it had been in three decades and the people desperate for a better life, General Ne Win called an emergency session of parliament to announce a plan intended to save the country. According to Sanda Win, one of Ne Win's daughters, her father believed that drastic measures were the only way to combat hyperinflation. During an interview with her during my first trip to Burma, she explained, "On the advice of his astrologers, my father changed the country's monetary system by substituting all the bank notes with bills divisible by the number nine—his lucky number."

Millions of Burmese woke up one morning to find that they were bankrupt, their life savings were worthless, and their country was financially ruined. Overnight, the mood of the people changed from what had been years of quiet resignation to vocal and violent rebellion. In the following months thousands of monks, students, and ordinary civilians took to the streets in protest against the government.

Several days before Daw Suu Kyi's arrival in Rangoon, at the end of March 1988, a student brawl in a local tea shop marked the transition toward what the military authorities believed was complete anarchy. In an effort to restore order, the authorities cracked down. In one pivotal incident, forty-one students were arrested for disorderly conduct and detained in a police van. All forty-one suffocated to death.

For weeks, as Daw Suu Kyi nursed her mother in the hospital, the violence intensified, with groups of young people marauding through the streets of Rangoon. Most of the protests were peaceful, but there were reports of looting and the destruction of public and private property. It was later estimated that over 60 percent of Rangoon's industrial base had been demolished during the civil unrest of 1988.

The revolt throughout the country was staged not only by city dwellers who had suffered under General Ne Win's repressive one-party political system, but also by ethnic minority groups and armed insurgents in the border areas who, for years, had been targets of brutality at the hands of Ne Win's army. At the same time, Aung San Suu Kyi had settled into a routine, going back and forth from the hospital each day to care for her mother.

By June, almost three months after Daw Suu Kyi arrived in Rangoon, the doctors announced that there was virtually no hope that her mother would ever recover. It was then that she made the decision to take Daw Khin Kyi home to University Avenue, where at least she would be in a familiar environment, and where she could die peacefully in her own room with views of Inya Lake. Several days after Daw Suu Kyi settled her mother in the house, the government under General Ne Win imposed a curfew. From six in the evening until six in the morning, anyone found in the streets could be either arrested or shot on sight.

The people rebelled even more. Civilians as well as soldiers, some dressed in uniform, others disguised in *longyis*, went on what later turned into a rampage of savagery and murder. The atmosphere was so chaotic that even close friends and family were wary of each other, each fearful that the others had been terrorized into acting as government informers.

Despite the series of foreign occupiers and military dictatorships that had controlled Burma for decades, the violence and anti-government unrest that erupted throughout the country in 1988 was something that had never before been seen.

*   *   *

Culture, religion, and tradition have always been sources of pride within Burmese society. Although nationalist spirit runs deep in the Burmese psyche, the country has been plagued by dissension and rebellion since its independence in 1948. The main source of political tension in Burma is the more than twenty different ethnic minority groups whose principal objective had always been greater autonomy or independence from a Burman-dominated central government.

The ancient method used by Burmese royalty to maintain unity was to create a kingdom whose power radiated out from the center of the realm to its fringes. The result was that, although there was absolute power and control at the center of the kingdom, the king was only a symbol of power in the rural and border areas.

At the end of the nineteenth century, the British colonized all of Burma. Putting the entire country under their direct or indirect control, the British also used the fringes against the center itself. By courting the minorities, recruiting hill people into their own armed units to control lowland Burmans, and even importing Indian soldiers to help keep the colony in line, the British created a precarious unity throughout the country. At the same time, the British encouraged considerable self-rule among different ethnic groups, such as the Chins, Kachins, Shans, Kayahs, and Karens.

In 1920, the National Schools in Burma were created in opposition to the Rangoon University Act, which limited higher education to only a small privileged class of students. The majority of the students who attended the National Schools were not only politically aware, but eventually instrumental in liberating Burma from British colonial control.

Aung San Suu Kyi has written that her father's desire to "free his country from foreign rule" lodged itself in Aung San's mind when he arrived at the National School in Yenangyaung. It was then that Aung San began to take an interest in the speeches of an international array of political leaders, as well as to learn the art of debating.

The youngest of six children, Aung San was born on February 13, 1915, in Natmauk, a small city in central Burma. For his entire life, he was described by most people who knew him—teachers, political colleagues, and family and friends—as intelligent, erratic, taciturn, aggressive, and totally committed to the cause of Burmese independence. Curiously, many of Aung San's own writings reveal that even as a small child he often conjured up stories in which he had magical powers that enabled him to drive the British out of his country.

During the early part of the twentieth century, a nationalist movement developed throughout Burma, influenced by concepts of nationalism, socialism, and communism coming out of Great Britain, Germany, and France.

In 1919, a major nationalist organization was formed—the General Council of Burmese Associations, or GCBA, which incorporated the Young Mens' Buddhist Association, which had been conducting nationalist educational activities since 1906.

In October 1930, Saya San, a physician and former member of the radical wing of the GCBA, founded another nationalist organization, the General Council of Buddhist Associations, whose members represented a wider constituency that included Hindus, Muslims, and Christians. Proclaiming himself king, Saya San set up a palace in the Tharrawaddy District, north of Rangoon, and began a strike against the occupying British forces. What became known in Burmese history as the "Saya San Rebellion" was, in part, an outcome of the terrible economic state of the villagers, exacerbated by the global economic depression in 1929 to 1930. Hard financial times led to escalating tensions, as Burmese farmers suffered from the declining price of rice on the open market, and Burmese laborers in the port cities suddenly found themselves competing with Indian immigrants for the few jobs available. In May 1930, a riot in Rangoon involving Burmese and Indian dockworkers marked the beginning of what would be a decade of violence between Burmese nationals and Indian and Chinese workers in Burma.

During the period of the Saya San Rebellion, another nationalist society calling itself the *Dobama Asiayone,* or "We Burmans Association," was formed in 1931 as a symbol of urban solidarity with the peasant revolt. To draw attention to themselves, the members began addressing each other as *Thakin* ("Master"), a term that was taboo in polite colonial society since the title was customarily used by Burmese as a respectful term of address for the British, much as the term "Sahib" was used in India.

The founders of the *Dobama Asiayone* appropriated the term *Thakin* as a way to persuade the Burmese to reject the slave mentality that the British had imposed, and instead, to adopt a master mentality of their own.

In 1931 in the Shan State, Saya San was captured by the British, and in 1932, his army, made up of peasant rebels armed with swords and spears, was eventually crushed by superior British forces. Although the Saya San Rebellion had never posed a real threat to British rule in Burma, it was a brutal war. Over 3,000 casualties (killed or wounded) were reported and 8,000 villagers arrested. The defeat of Saya San became an inspiration to the Burmese people, and eventually the impetus needed to organize nationalist groups that would challenge British domination.

The same year that the Saya San Rebellion was put down by the British, Aung San entered Rangoon University. Inspired by Saya San's courage, Aung San was only one of a group of young nationals at the university who would follow Saya San's example of military force as the only way to achieve independence. According to a Burmese scholar who knew Aung San during their university days, the future general was a "voracious reader," and "committed to learning as much as he could about language, religion, and politics."

Professor Khynt Maung of Yangon University describes his first meeting with Aung San nearly sixty-five years ago. "He was an intellectual by instinct," the professor begins, "and yet, at the same time, he could be totally undisciplined. I knew him well and I knew people who were quite involved in his activities, and most said of him that he was extremely rude and very unpredictable. But, of course, he was a genius so people accepted his idiosyncrasies."

In 1938, Aung San left the University of Rangoon and joined the *Dobama Asiayone*. Within months, the society split into two sections as a result of internal disputes. Aung San went with the majority faction led by Thakin Kodaw Hmaing. Up until then, with the exception of Aung San and his colleagues, most students at Rangoon University had little interest in politics. Given the global depression, the students were more concerned about mastering English, passing exams, and finding good jobs after graduation. It wasn't until they realized that the competitive examination system was being weighted against Burmese nationals, in favor of British subjects—which ultimately would affect the possibility of finding jobs—that students as well as university graduates began to take an active interest in anti-British activities.

Before long, Rangoon University became the center of power for the *Dobama Asiayone*, which became the symbol of rebellion against the British. Students as well as the general public began referring to the members of the group as *Thakins*.

In the autumn of 1935, U Nu was elected president of the Rangoon University Students Union, or RUSU, and Aung San was elected its secretary. Not only was the RUSU used as a forum for discussing national issues, it was also the platform on which three men would be brought to national prominence, and who would later play central roles in Burma's struggle for independence.

They were Aung San, who was to lead Burma to independence; U Nu, who was to become the country's first democratically elected prime minister; and Shu Maung, who would become better known by his *nom de guerre*, Ne Win, or "Brilliant Like the Sun."

In 1936, one of the founders of the group established the *Nagani* or Red Dragon book club in order to publish and distribute socialist and Marxist literature. Deviating from the club's usual format, Thakin Nu, later known as U Nu, got into trouble when he published an article calling for the dismissal of a Burmese member of the faculty for "alleged moral improprieties." In response, British authorities not only expelled Thakin Nu from the university, but also Aung San, who had functioned as the newspaper's editor. Although the incident was technically a university matter, it nonetheless provoked a student strike that quickly escalated to include wider political issues such as Burmese independence.

Student demonstrations broke out within the university complex, spreading quickly to include the support of Rangoon-area high school students who, as a group, had formed the All Burma Student Union. In order to avoid what threatened to become widespread civil disorder, British authorities agreed to re-admit Thakin Nu and Thakin Aung San to the university. By then, both men had already committed themselves to full-time political careers.

During the 1936 election, the *Thakins* succeeded in having two of their members elected to the legislature. In 1938, the *Thakins* promptly began organizing dockworkers and oil field workers, eventually leading a march of striking oil refinery workers from Syriam to Rangoon. When a student was killed by police during the demonstrations, a second university strike was called. In February 1939, tensions escalated when seventeen students and monks were killed during a protest in Mandalay.

Although predominantly socialist in their basic ideology, the *Thakins* had no specific political platform. Highly eclectic, the group was influenced by several different political parties and philosophies, including Sun Zhongshan (Sun Yat-sen), the Indian National Congress, European and Japanese fascism, and the Irish Sinn Fein movement. Regardless of fragmented political thought, the *Thakins* were the first group to call for independence since Saya San and his army had fought for an independent Burmese nation.

Ba Maw and U Saw, two Burmese opposition leaders, suddenly found themselves pushed from the center of political attention. Although not enamored of the British, both Ba Maw and U Saw were far more conventional than the *Thakins*, and had a bigger stake in the political system established by the colonial government.

It was the students, however, who became the prominent voice of protest, operating largely outside the established political process. Unlike the monks, who had entered politics in order to defend religion, the *Thakins* were secular—particularly Aung San, who defined independence in terms of "Burmese" rather than majority "Burman" nationalism. In fact, the *Thakins* maintained close relations with the Indian National Congress and even attempted to defuse communal tensions after the anti-Indian riot of 1938. What they did not abandon, however, was tradition. One of the founders of the *Dobama Asiayone*, and one of

the leaders who had the greatest influence on Aung San, was
Thakin Kodaw Hmaing, a former Buddhist monk and writer
who at the age of ten had witnessed the exile of the Burmese
king and queen from Mandalay. Described by scholars as a living historical link between the Burmese revolution and the cultural traditions of the pre-British Burmese kingdom, Thakin
Kodaw Hmaing combined western democratic and socialist
thought with Buddhist themes. One of his most famous texts
deals with what he described as an earthly nirvana or paradise
that was lost because men had become greedy and acquisitive
and were no longer capable of governing themselves—the reason
a Buddha had been elected as their sovereign.

That particular theme was not incompatible with what
Thakin U Nu had always argued—specifically, that "capitalism
engendering greed precluded the attainment of salvation . . . and
in a socialist society the promotion of the people's welfare was
not only a meritorious act for the ruler but it also enabled the
masses to turn from material concerns to the attainment of
their own spiritual enlightenment." Even the left wing of the
Thakin movement, led by Thakin Soe and Thakin Than Tun,
drew on Buddhist concepts as a way of introducing the Burmese
peoples to a Marxist philosophy.

In February 1939, Ba Maw was replaced as prime minister by
Tharrawaddy U Pu. In September of that same year, war broke
out in Europe, and Ba Maw's Sinyetha Party joined forces with
the Burma Revolutionary Party, another *Thakin* group formed
by Kodaw Hmaing and Aung San that eventually became known
as the Freedom Bloc, a coalition committed to full Burmese independence. In this year, too, Aung San was a founding member
of the Communist Party of Burma, an organization he subsequently left.

In September 1940, U Pu's government was replaced by one
formed by U Saw, head of the Myochit Patriot Party. Described
by historian Frank Trager, an expert on Southeast Asia, as a
"strange self-educated uncouth leader who had won a following
among the peasant masses," U Saw attempted to suppress the

activity of Aung San's Freedom Bloc Party by persuading the British to grant Burma full self-governing or dominion status. It was a move on U Saw's part that would put him in a more powerful position, rather than ensure independence for the Burmese people.

During World War II, the allied proclamation contained in the Atlantic Charter in August 1941 guaranteed "the right of all peoples to choose the form of government under which they live." Burmese nationalists were suddenly hopeful. Hope was replaced by bitter disappointment the following month, however, when Prime Minister Winston Churchill qualified that proclamation in an address before British Parliament when he announced that it did not apply to Burma, which had its own "program of political evolution."

In response, U Saw went to London to argue for dominion status for Burma. Not only was he unsuccessful, but he was arrested by the British on his way back to Rangoon, and charged with attempting to make contact with the Japanese. Exiled to Uganda, he remained there until the end of the war.

A number of historians have suggested that had the Churchill government been more flexible on the issue of self-government, Burma would have fought on the side of the Allies during the war. In fact, in his memoir, *Breakthrough in Burma*, Ba Maw writes of his bitterness when he realized that the principles of the Atlantic Charter applied only to "white" nations such as Poland, but not to non-white colonial peoples like the Burmese. One of the reasons that the Burmese were favorably disposed toward the Japanese was that Japanese propaganda called for a common Asian struggle against "white imperialism." For Burmese nationalists, however, it was never a choice between Britain and Japan as occupiers, but rather choosing the alliance that was the quickest way to full independence.

During the war years, the Japanese military became interested in Burma not only because of its natural resources, particularly oil, but also because the Burma Road had always provided a route through which the Allies could supply the Chiang Kai-shek government in China. According to historical accounts by the Chinese government during that period, the only way to have a speedy and successful end to the war between Japan and China was by cutting off that route.

In 1939, Japanese agents contacted Ba Maw who, during the preceding year, had already discussed the possibility of getting Japanese support for his Freedom Bloc ally, Thakin Aung San. In August 1940, in conjunction with Japanese advances into Southeast Asia, Aung San was smuggled by ship out of Burma into Tokyo by the Japanese to lay the groundwork for armed struggle against the British. Under the leadership of a Japanese Army colonel, Suzuki Keiji, an intelligence organization called the *Minami Kikan* was established by the Japanese military to coordinate operations in Burma.

After Aung San returned to Burma, he contacted the *Thakins* and arranged to sneak thirty members of the group, including himself, out of the country. The plan was that the group, called the Thirty Comrades, would receive military training from the Japanese on Hainan Island off the south coast of China. Along with two hundred Burmese who were living in Thailand and Japanese members of the *Minami Kikan* under the command of Colonel Suzuki, the Thirty Comrades would become the core of the Burma Independence Army, or BIA, established in Bangkok in late December 1941.

In January 1942, when Japanese forces began the invasion of the Tenasserium area along the Andaman Sea and other parts of Lower Burma, the BIA aided them in their advance by engaging retreating British forces in combat. One of the Thirty Comrades, Thakin Shu Maung, eventually known as Ne Win, infiltrated Rangoon in early February and organized sabotage activities. In March 1942, Rangoon fell to the Japanese, and British troops evacuated Mandalay. In May, the Burma Road was cut off.

Aung San and many of his soldiers contracted malaria during the march with the BIA, and those who did not succumb to the disease landed in Rangoon General Hospital, where they were treated. Although he was only twenty-seven years old, Aung San already had a reputation throughout Burma as a hero—the reason that several doctors and senior nurses decided that it was not fitting for a junior staff member to care for him. An attractive woman named Khin Kyi, a senior nurse and one of the most respected caretakers at the hospital, was elected to tend to General Aung San. Before long, respect turned to affection and soon became love for the general and the nurse.

In August 1942, when most of Burma was still in Japanese hands, the Japanese appointed Ba Maw as Prime Minister, Thakin Nu as Minister of Foreign Affairs, and Aung San as Minister of Defense and Commander of the new 4,000-strong Burma Defense Army. In January 1943, Japanese Prime Minister Tojo Hideki announced that independence would be granted to Burma by the end of the year. The reality, however, was that Ba Maw's government was only nominally independent, and Burma was seen by Tokyo primarily as an economic and strategic component of its all-out war effort.

In March 1943, when Aung San traveled to Tokyo to be decorated by the Emperor, it was his old colleague Colonel Suzuki who told him of Japan's true intentions concerning Burmese independence. Eventually, the Japanese colonel was disgraced for his alleged pro-Burmese position.

Despite Aung San's profound commitment and active fight for an independent Burma, he managed to find the time to marry the woman he loved. On September 6, 1942, Daw Khin Kyi and Aung San were married in Rangoon.

It wasn't long before Daw Khin Kyi realized that she had married not only a national hero, but also the country's destiny. Although Aung San was a loving husband and a devoted father to his two sons and his daughter, he spent much of his time away from home.

8

Burmese life under the Japanese military authorities was harsh. Thousands of Burmese were forced into labor battalions, and the *Kempetai*, or Japanese military police, were hated and feared. Although Ba Maw disliked the Thakins, and especially disliked Aung San, when he learned that the group was planning armed resistance against the Japanese, he did not betray them.

In August and September 1944, Aung San along with the communist leader Thakin Than Tun, had already established contact with allied forces, and held a series of secret meetings with Burma National Army officers and several groups of socialists and communists. During those meetings, concrete resistance plans against the Japanese were made. By the end of September, the Anti-Fascist Organization, later to become the Anti-Fascist People's Freedom League, or AFPFL, was created. It was Aung San who played the central role when it came to coordinating diverse groups within the party, such as the Karen National Organization, the Japanese-sponsored East Asia Youth League, former associates from *Dobama Asiayone*, as well as Burmese socialists and communists. Aung San's biggest accomplishment, however, was to win the support of Great Britain's Lord Louis Mountbatten, head of the Southeast Asia Command, which was now poised to re-invade Burma.

Despite the Burma National Army's initial collaboration with the Japanese, Lord Mountbatten was inclined to forgive and forget the events of 1942. As far as he was concerned, it was more important to secure the cooperation of the BNA so that Great Britain could regain control of Burma from the Japanese. Many other allied officers, however, regarded Aung San as an opportunist who changed sides only when the British and Americans regained the upper hand.

On March 27, after receiving a prearranged signal from Lord Mountbatten, Aung San and his soldiers began attacking Japanese units in tandem with the allied advance. In early May, Rangoon was captured, although sporadic fighting continued in various parts of the country even after the Japanese surrender on August 15, 1945.

At the end of May 1945, the BNA was officially recognized as a component of the British Allied Forces and renamed the Patriotic Burmese Forces, or PBF. At victory celebrations held in Rangoon in June, the "resistance flag" of the Anti-Fascist Organization—a white star on a red field—flew alongside the Union Jack. Finally, Lord Mountbatten and other British commanders had come to respect General Aung San's commitment to independence, and to view him as the principal representative of Burmese national aspirations.

In London and India, however, where the British government of Burma had been in exile during the war, attitudes were quite different. Not only did the exiled British government still consider Aung San to be a turncoat who—if it was up to them— would have no role to play in future developments, but British officials in London also disagreed amongst themselves concerning the postwar political status of Burma.

On May 17, 1945, the Churchill government issued a "white paper" on Burma that proposed a very conservative program: the 1937 constitution with its elected prime minister would be suspended, and a British governor, appointed in London, would retain all authority. As a gesture of compromise, however, the British agreed to give the section of the country called

"Burma Proper," populated predominantly by Burmans, "full self-government within the Commonwealth" after 1948.

The Shan state and the other border regions inhabited by non-Burman minorities would remain under British rule indefinitely. The white paper also called for several years of economic reconstruction for war-ravaged Burma, which the pre-war colonial construction companies would be in charge of implementing. The reality was that to many citizens the white paper granted the Burmese under the British even less freedom than the country had had under Japanese occupation.

Confident that his party, the AFPFL, had a broad base of support even among the socialist and communist parties, as well as control over a large number of armed soldiers, Aung San initiated an active campaign against the white paper. At a mass meeting in Rangoon on August 19, 1945, Aung San demanded that the British grant Burma immediate independence. By December 1945, Aung San was in command of more than 4,700 men who had been absorbed into the regular armed forces, and another 3,500 that comprised what was called the People's Volunteer Organization, or PVO, which eventually became the private army of the AFPFL. Establishing contingents throughout the country, the PVO eventually had an army of more than 14,000 men. For the British, the situation was suddenly serious.

In an attempt to diffuse the power of the AFPFL, Reginald Dorman-Smith, the British governor who had headed the pre-war colonial government, enlisted the support of U Saw, who had returned from exile in Uganda. Excluding AFPFL members from his executive council, Dorman-Smith included U Saw as well as the conservative Sir Paw Tun. Conditions within the AFPFL became chaotic when Thakin Than Tun, still an avowed communist, organized mass demonstrations and guerrilla operations to topple the Dorman-Smith government.

In January 1946, General Aung San went to Myitkyina in an effort to gain the support of Kachin chiefs, another ethnic minority. Successful, in March Aung San promptly organized the first Panglong Conference, which was attended by representatives from the Shan, Karens, Kachins, and Chins. U Nu, who would become the country's first democratically elected prime minister, was chosen to represent the Anti-Fascist People's Freedom League. Unfortunately, during U Nu's speech, he managed to alienate many of the minority groups when he claimed that it was the British who had fostered ethnic divisions as a result of their separation of Burma Proper from the border areas. Nevertheless, in response to the British white paper that called for, among other provisions, separate minority areas, the AFPFL reasserted its position that the Burmans and minority peoples should unite to form a single state. Proclaiming his own liberal concept, Aung San stated that the basis of a nation was not "race or culture but a feeling of oneness that develops as different peoples share hardship and prosperity in common."

In September 1946, a general strike broke out involving government workers, police, laborers, and university and high school students. Seeing no alternative, the British removed Dorman-Smith from office and replaced him with Hubert Rance. All too aware that there were limited British troops at his disposal, Rance was forced to come to an agreement with General Aung San. The result was that an eleven-member executive council was formed, six of whom were picked from the ranks of the AFPFL, while General Aung San was appointed its deputy chairman.

On October 2, 1946, the general strike ended. But the trouble was far from over.

Immediately following Governor Rance's decision to include Aung San in the government, the communists, while members of the AFPFL, were following their own agenda actually under the leadership of Thakin Than Tun. They labeled Aung San a collaborationist. In retaliation, Aung San expelled Than Tun and several of his loyalists from the AFPFL.

The British government in London, under Labour Prime Minister Clement Attlee, was apparently encouraged enough by Aung San's break with the communists to believe that he was the best person with whom to negotiate. In December 1946, Attlee invited Aung San and other political leaders to London.

On January 27, 1947, Prime Minister Attlee and General Aung San signed an agreement calling for full independence within a year, elections for a constituent assembly within four months, continued British aid, British sponsorship of Burma to membership in international organizations, and most significantly, the promise that the border areas would be included within the boundaries of the new nation.

Supported by the anti-colonial principles of a postwar British Labour Party government, Aung San became the architect of Burma's independence. Envisioning a union in which formerly separated peoples would be joined in a framework providing for a substantial degree of diversity, he won the agreement from the leaders of several important ethnic groups—Shan, Chin, and Kachin—that they would join with the interim Burmese government. The Karen group, however, declined and believed they were never properly consulted.

The situation of the Karens was somewhat different from that of the other minorities. Tribal peoples who had migrated from southern China around the sixth or seventh century AD, the Karen nationality was in part developed through Christian missionary activity that encouraged a feeling of a separate national identity, quite distinct from the world and the philosophies of the Buddhist Burmans or Mons. Memories of harsh treatment under the Burmese kings led Karen leaders to form the National Karen Association in 1881, which promoted Karen unity.

The Karen role in the British armed forces in Burma was also instrumental in their identifying with the British. Further, the Karens had been treated harshly by the BIA during the Japanese takeover, and a large number of them had been executed as British sympathizers. After World War II, many Karen leaders began campaigning for the establishment of an independent Karen state within the British Commonwealth—separate from Burma.

During and after the war, Aung San had been diligent in forging links with minority leaders, including even some of those within the Karen group. Although the AFPFL included minority groups, most preferred keeping a separate identity to becoming part of an independent Burma. "A nation," Aung San said, "is a conglomeration of races and religions that should develop a nationalism that is common with the welfare of one and all, irrespective of race, religion, class, or sex."

The agreement that was signed on January 27, 1947, between the British government and the Burmese nationalists, united Burma Proper with the border areas. As a result of that agreement, a second conference was held at Panglong between February 7 and 12, 1947, during which provisions were made for a new Kachin state to be established in the north of the country, the autonomy of the Shan to be recognized within a separate Shan state, and the Chins to join independent Burma on the condition that they would receive financial aid from the government to build up their area.

In accordance with the second Panglong agreement, the Shan and Kachin states were created. Shortly after that, a Karenni delegation was seated in the Constituent Assembly. This led to the establishment of a Karenni state, which eventually became the Kayah State in 1951. The second Panglong conference, while settling the question of most border areas, rejected the Karen National Union's proposal that a separate Karen state be established in both the Delta region and Thai borderlands. In retaliation, the Karens boycotted elections for the Constituent Assembly scheduled for that April.

When elections were held for the Constituent Assembly, there was a total of 255 seats, with Burma Proper being allotted 210, with 24 reserved for the Karens and 4 for Anglo-Burmans, while the border areas were allotted 45. The AFPFL won an overwhelming victory within the Burmese Assembly with 248 representatives elected, most of whom were socialists or members of the PVO.

On June 9, 1947, the assembly met for the first time. Thakin Nu was elected President of the Constituent Assembly.

On the morning of July 19, 1947, gunmen entered the secretariat building in central Rangoon and murdered Aung San and seven of his ministers, including his eldest brother, Ba Win.

Excluded from the political process after the January 1947 Attlee–Aung San agreement, it is generally believed that U Saw had plotted the assassination, convinced that with Aung San out of the way, the British governor would turn to him to lead the country. Later, authorities discovered that he had also been plotting an alternative takeover, which would have been by force. The crime was poorly planned, which enabled the police to trace the gunmen to U Saw's house where he and his accomplices were immediately arrested.

At a special tribunal held in October through December 1947, U Saw and his accomplices were tried and convicted of murdering Aung San. They were executed in May 1948.

Daw Khin Kyi, Aung San Suu Kyi's mother, was a symbol of strength and dignity after the assassination of her husband, an event that was not only a personal loss, but also a national tragedy. The violent death of Aung San, the architect of Burma's independence, at thirty-two years old, stunned the nation.

All that had been carefully constructed now seemed on the verge of collapse. Governor Rance, however, was determined not to use the assassination as a pretext to delay the independence process. He immediately appointed Thakin Nu as prime minister.

On September 24, 1947, the Constituent Assembly approved the first constitution of the independent Union of Burma, providing for a parliamentary system of government and a bicameral legislature. The upper house, the Chamber of Nationalities, had strong minority representation—72 out of 125 members were non-Burman—while the lower house, or the Chamber of Deputies, was elected from a geographical section of constituents, based on population. Still, when it came to granting minorities their rights, it was filled with ambiguities.

For example, the Shan and Karenni states were given the right to secede from the union after ten years, while the Mon and Rakhine states ended up without any territory at all. Yet, at the same time as leaders of the Shan and Karenni states were allowed to retain their feudal control, a complicated set of regulations determined that ethnic Burmans would have the majority rule in both their houses of parliament, which in essence assured a majority Burman vote.

After a Karenni delegation was finally seated in the Constituent Assembly, a Karenni state was promised, and later to be renamed the Kayah State. On the western frontier, while the Chins were not granted a state, they were given what was called a "Chin Special Division." Also confusing was that the promised separate Karenni State remained without clear borders and, in fact, right up until independence, arguments were heard over the merits of "national states," versus "communal seats" in parliament, as opposed to special "ethnic minority rights." Although a Karenni state was not set up, a referendum was promised and, in return, the Karen Affairs Council agreed "To aid and advise the Union Government on matters relating to the Karens."

Also written into the 1947 constitution was that the prime minister was responsible to the Assembly, while the President of the Union of Burma had only ceremonial powers as head of state. The most positive aspect of the constitution provided for a "commitment to social justice and the establishment of a welfare state." The rights of people to employment, education, support in old age, and health care were provided for, and although the right of private property was recognized, large absentee land holdings were prohibited. Further, the state had the ultimate right to own and distribute land, and while officially secular, freedom of religion was nonetheless guaranteed. Other fundamental civil rights included freedom of speech and assembly, equality between the sexes, and equality before the law.

On October 17, 1947, Prime Minister U Nu and Prime Minister Clement Attlee signed a treaty formally recognizing the independence of the Union of Burma.

On December 1, 1947, the British parliament, over the strenuous objection of Churchill's Conservative Party, passed the Burma Independence Act. The date for the transfer of power was set for January 4, 1948.

The fact that independence was ultimately achieved with a minimum of violence was a tribute to the moderation of the Anti-Fascist People's Freedom League and British leaders from the Labour Party.

Burma became independent on January 4, 1948—a tribute to the determination and sacrifice of General Aung San.

* * *

Postcolonial leaders such as General Aung San and Prime Minister U Nu each had brief moments of success in uniting the country. Even in the flush of independence from the British, communist and secession leaders, mostly in the mountain regions, continued to plan their own campaigns for self-determination that ultimately destroyed any plan for national unity.

The Communist Party of Burma (CPB) went underground in March 1948. Shortly afterward, many ethnic Burman and Karen units in the army rebelled, eventually making their border areas geographically and culturally impossible for the central government to control. In 1949, the Karen National Union (KNU) went underground, followed by other ethnic minorities, including the Mons, Pad, Rakhines, and Karennis. At one point during that time, control of the country by the central government was limited to just six miles out of Rangoon.

In the mid-1950s, factional disputes broke out throughout Burma between political parties in urban areas as well as between political rivals in rural villages. Once again, the main concern of the central government was to prevent the fighting from splitting the country into different ethnic groups and regions.

Faced with a military coup, on October 28, 1958, Prime Minister U Nu put forward a motion in the Chamber of Deputies in order to ensure that the government was strong enough to keep the country together. Calling on General Ne Win, a former colleague from the days when Burma was fighting for independence from the British, he asked him to take charge of a caretaker government. "It is the only way to save Burma from complete civil insurrection and anarchy," U Nu told the people.

In his acceptance speech before parliament, General Ne Win stated, "I promise to do my best to hold fair and free elections within six months, if the insurgency and crimes are brought to an end within that period of time."

Within days, Ne Win formed a new cabinet comprised almost exclusively of civil servants whose sole purpose was to reestablish law and order throughout the country. At the same time, General Ne Win not only issued an ultimatum to thousands of rebels to surrender to his troops or face execution, he also ordered the arrest of hundreds of politicians.

Next on General Ne Win's agenda was to restore order within all government offices, enterprises, and services. To accomplish this, he created the Defense Services Institute which, under the direction of a capable and dynamic subordinate named Brigadier Aung Gyi, would control all the state-owned industrial and commercial enterprises. Within a short time, the Defense Services Institute was operating a large economic complex that included banks, factories, shipping, and numerous other commercial enterprises, some of which had been taken over from private control, while others had been established under the direction of Brigadier Aung Gyi.

General Ne Win also changed the administration of the border areas where various ethnic groups lived, making them subject to the same laws that governed the rest of the country for the first time in Burma's history. As a result, the hereditary chiefs of the Shan and Kayah states, to name just two, were forced to surrender substantial political power, as well as large financial revenues that they had collected and held in accordance with the 1947 constitution envisaged by General Aung San.

In a harbinger of things to come, Ne Win's caretaker regime, rather than form its own political party, established the National Solidarity Association, an organization composed only of the military. In his own defense, General Ne Win claimed that it was the only way to ensure cooperation between the military and civilian populations in towns and villages throughout Burma. Only then, he told the people, could there be a demonstration of loyalty to the state, which in turn would translate into unity throughout the country.

In February 1960, General Ne Win kept his promise and began the process of reinstating the civilian government by holding elections for parliament. U Nu, the former prime minister and the most well-known candidate in the elections, based his campaign platform on the issue of democracy versus fascism, and on the promise to establish Buddhism as the state religion. He also hinted at the possibility of granting autonomy to the Mon and the Arakanese, two other ethnic states.

For the first time in Burma's history, more than half the electorate turned out to vote. The result was an overwhelming victory once again for U Nu.

On April 4, 1960, U Nu took office as prime minister, and immediately reorganized his party, renaming it the *Pyidaungsu*, or Union League Party.

Typical of the constant ambiguity between the civil and the military, the National Solidarity Association, under General Ne Win, continued to exist.

In February 1962, Prime Minister U Nu convened a conference in Rangoon between his central government and ethnic minority leaders to discuss their political demands. One of the major points on his agenda was to propose that a new constitution be written to provide for "pure federalism," and which would replace the constitution that had been written in 1947 by General Aung San. The country was changing, Prime Minister U Nu claimed. The old constitution was no longer relevant.

The reaction from the majority of Burmans was alarm that eventually resulted in a bitter split in Prime Minister U Nu's own party. In fact, arguments concerning the possibility of allowing various ethnic groups to have their own independent or autonomous states produced such severe internal conflict that during U Nu's National Party congress in January 1962, there was a general crisis of confidence. Politicians who had been allies of Prime Minister U Nu suddenly accused him of ruining the economy and of running the government inefficiently, while the business community voiced their opposition at his announced decision to nationalize all foreign trade as of March 1, 1962. Resistance from the military was even stronger, with particular objections to the idea of "pure federalism."

On March 2, 1962, the military under General Ne Win seized power.

Almost immediately, prominent political leaders, including U Nu, were arrested and held without trial, the 1947 constitution was suspended, and parliament was dissolved. By a collective decision of the Revolutionary Council, General Ne Win became "supreme legislative, executive, and judicial authority."

In one of his first official acts as supreme head of the country, Ne Win left for China on a state visit. Upon his return, he claimed that he had been so impressed with Chairman Mao that he intended to implement a socialist system in Burma—Burmese style. On April 30, 1962, Ne Win officially created the Burmese Way to Socialism, a program that was neither socialism nor communism nor capitalism, but rather proof of his profound xenophobia and superstition.

Under the guise of cultural integrity, General Ne Win sealed off Burma from the rest of the world, plunging the country deep into economic despair and the people into abject poverty. Statistics gathered from the International Monetary Fund in Washington, D.C., in 1995, report that the per capita income during Ne Win's regime was $200 per year, one of the lowest in the world. Ironically, under the current SLORC regime, the per capita income is still $200 per year.

The Burmese Way to Socialism program outlined its long-range goals in a twenty-one-point basic policy agenda. The main point of the program was its commitment to building a new nation for "We, the working people of the national races of the Union of Burma." One central objective was the creation of a socialist economy—the "planned, proportional development of all the national productive forces, aimed at eliminating the exploitation of man by man and creating a more prosperous and morally better society." In that spirit of improvement, General Ne Win announced a clean break with the parliamentary institutions of the past. It was the beginning of Burma's descent into third-world status.

Although Ne Win claimed that his intention was to establish a collective society for the benefit of the people, the reality was quite another story. Almost immediately after seizing power, he set up a central revolutionary council, division councils, and town and village councils, all of which were dominated by the military, and which reached out from Rangoon to the entire country. Eventually, the Burmese Army and Ne Win's Burmese Socialist Program Party became indistinguishable.

On the record, the "Burmese Way" stated that "parliamentary democracy has been tried and tested in furtherance of the aims of socialist development." According to Ne Win, however, Burma's "parliamentary democracy" had not only "failed to serve our socialist development, but . . . lost sight of and deviated from the socialist aims." The council promised to establish "mass and class organizations" based "primarily on the strength of peasants and other working masses who form the great majority of the nation." But instead of employing the "working masses" in the cultivation of Burma's natural resources such as teak, diamonds, rubies, jade, emeralds, sapphires, and food crops and minerals from the rich soil, Ne Win poured all the country's revenue into the army.

For the entire time that Ne Win was in power, the army waged war against more than a dozen different ethnic minorities, as well as against the Communist Party of Burma, which controlled many of the prize opium-growing areas in the mountains of Shan State. Ironically, despite Ne Win's open admiration for Chairman Mao, the main opposition to his government was the communists funded almost exclusively by China. In March 1964, General Ne Win banned all political parties except his, and Burma became a one-party state.

In November 1969, in an attempt by the Revolutionary Council to transform the Burmese Socialist Program Party from a cadre to a mass party, a new constitution was drafted. Included in its bylaws were precise definitions of how the party was to be organized on the regional and local levels, as well as requirements for party membership, and specific intraparty decision-making procedures based on "democratic centralism." Under those guidelines it was clear that ethnic regions or states would never gain their autonomy.

Still, Ne Win was obliged to try and keep peace in the rural areas of the country by somehow making the ethnic groups adhere to the laws of the central government. Armed ethnic resistance only increased after the military's seizure of power, but during the 1969 party seminar, Ne Win declared, "Our Union is just one homogeneous whole. Someone from the Chin State, for instance, can go wherever he likes within the Union and stay wherever he likes. So, too, a Burmese. Everyone can take part in any of the affairs, whether political, economic, administrative, or judicial. He can choose his own role." Given these new guidelines, Ne Win summed up what would be his political platform. "We will not need to have separate governments within the Union."

At the first party congress, held in June to July 1971, the party constitution was officially adopted. A committee was set up and headed by Brigadier San Yu, a member of the Revolutionary Council, whose purpose was to draft the new state constitution.

While General Ne Win promised a transition from rule by a "close-knit military elite" to that of a "socialist democracy," his reasons for establishing the Revolutionary Council, he said, were solely to win a broader base of popular participation. In April 1972, in a meaningless gesture of commitment to the new constitution, General Ne Win and twenty other military leaders resigned their commissions. Within hours, Ne Win proclaimed himself Prime Minister and head of the Burmese Socialist Program Party.

In October 1973, the second congress was held, during which the committee's draft constitution was approved.

On January 3, 1974, the constitution was finally declared valid.

On March 2, 1974, the Revolutionary Council, adhering to an order given by General Ne Win, was formally dissolved, and power was officially transferred to the newly elected People's Assembly. In yet another incarnation, General Ne Win, known as Prime Minister Ne Win, who also held the title of Chief of the Armed Forces, became the first president of the new Socialist Republic of the Union of Burma.

One of the most significant points in the 1974 constitution is in its preamble, which states the new socialist republic's commitment to "socialist democracy," and a "socialist economic system." It was a curious interpretation of the reality, since the constitution recognized only one political party, the Burmese Socialist Program Party.

Insurgency by ethnic minorities and members of the outlawed Burmese Communist Party continued in many parts of the country, especially in the border regions adjoining China, Laos, and Thailand. Many of these groups engaged in drug trafficking, notably in Shan State smuggling, and other illicit activities as a means of support, while other minority groups, under local warlords, supplied what had already become a thriving black market.

In 1983, in an atmosphere of dissension and an unhealthy economy, Union Day celebrations in Rangoon drew delegates from Burma's more than sixty disparate national groups to the nation's capital to participate in government-organized ceremonies. Posters marking the occasion emphasized the spirit of unity among the varied groups. To many observers, there was no better reminder that an absence of national solidarity in Burma, or cultural unity, was still the country's fundamental problem.

9

YEARS LATER, Aung San Suu Kyi would look back on that time in 1988 when she arrived in Rangoon to care for her dying mother and realized she was beginning to understand what her father really meant to the country. "The advantage of being somebody in a democratic party is that you don't really have to prepare yourself as an individual for such responsibility because you are not going to be a dictator. You are going to be working as part of a team. Although Aung San died, the independence to which he had dedicated his life came to his country."

Aung San Suu Kyi has never claimed that when she came to Burma in 1988, it was to lead a pro-democracy movement. "It wasn't as if the students were organized in definite political groups in 1988," Daw Suu Kyi explains. "The democracy movement evolved out of general chaos that was everywhere in Burma. It was this climate of rebellion that caused many political groups to emerge, which eventually coalesced into a democracy movement."

A prominent Burmese, whom I will call William, who has opposed the government for decades and was sentenced to six years in the notorious Insein Prison by the SLORC, offers this analysis: "Suu Kyi arrived in Rangoon in 1988 with the sole intention of caring for her mother, and returning to her family in England.

There was never any question that she came to Rangoon to lead a pro-democracy government. What is democracy to a small Southeast Asian third-world nation? After all, the Burmese people have never known freedom and have lived under three brutal military regimes. The beginning of the democratic movement was borne out of frustration and anger at Ne Win. It wasn't until much later that democracy become part of the people's lexicon."

Whether General Ne Win was afraid that internal chaos would provide Burma's powerful neighbors—China and India—the opportunity to create more chaos, or whether he imagined that his army would implode on itself, he soon realized that from the military old-guard's perspective the situation was uncontrollable.

In July 1988, as the demonstrations and unrest spread and people began clamoring for a change, General Ne Win called another emergency session of parliament. At the time, the consensus was that Ne Win would propose a referendum for a multiparty system of government, if for nothing other than to calm the people's wrath over the desperate economic situation. In a lengthy speech, however, Ne Win surprised the military and the entire country by announcing his intention to retire to spend more time with his children and grandchildren. "The world is changing," he told the stunned audience, "and what we have done has made the country suffer. As chairman of the party I am responsible, and so I offer my resignation. I am leaving the party and leaving politics." Despite his alleged concern for the welfare of the people, General Ne Win's political party, the Burmese Socialist Program Party, was not quite ready to relinquish control. In July 1988, Sein Lwin, a loyalist to Ne Win, replaced him. It was an incendiary choice, as it was Sein Lwin whom many citizens held responsible for the death of unarmed demonstrators in March, when the protests started.

On August 8, 1988, a day known in recent Burmese history as the "Four 8s," a nationwide strike was called that included students, civilians, lawyers, doctors, monks, and civil servants. Convinced that the resignation of Ne Win meant that Burma would finally be liberated from one-party rule, crowds surged into the streets in a euphoria of countrywide pro-democracy demonstration. Once again, Sein Lwin responded by ordering troops to open fire. Within hours, Burma was once again under martial law.

The demonstrations, however, continued and the death toll mounted. There were incidents, too, of suspected military informers being killed by mob justice. As Daw Suu Kyi nursed her dying mother, she was kept informed daily of the bloodshed and, along with everyone else, mourned those who lost their lives on the streets of Burmese cities. By then, rumors that Daw Suu Kyi was in the country had already spread.

In an atmosphere where speculation and heresy are often taken as fact, superstition considered scientific, and symbols and numbers transformed into concrete realities, many people believed that the presence of General Aung San's daughter in Burma meant that more than fifty years of repression, civil unrest, and violence would finally end.

All throughout the city of Rangoon, pictures of General Aung San became a prominent symbol of the pro-democracy movement. Typical of the contradictions so inherent in Burmese culture, the military also considered General Aung San their revered symbol, since he had founded the army. What the Burmese people could not know at the time was that 1988 was the beginning of a new chapter in the country's history.

In a desperate attempt to maintain control, the military removed Sein Lwin from office and replaced him with a civilian, Dr. Maung Maung, who was another loyalist to Ne Win, and who became the new president and chairman of the Burmese Socialist Program Party. For the first time since Prime Minister U Nu had been elected, Burma had a civilian head of government.

In response to the hundreds of thousands of people who continued to demonstrate throughout the country, Dr. Maung Maung tried a new tactic. He lifted martial law and promised a referendum. Once again, the people believed that Burma would finally have democracy. Two student leaders, Min Ko Naing and Moe Thi Zun, became prominent figures in the struggle for multiparty democratic rule by working tirelessly for months behind the scenes. Other figures came to the fore, including ex-general Tin U, a former Minister of Defense, and Bohmy Aung who, like General Ne Win and Aung San, was one of the original Thirty Comrades. It was at the invitation of such figures that Daw Suu Kyi finally intervened with an open letter to the government proposing that a committee—with no ties to the military—be formed for the sole purpose of leading the country toward multiparty elections. It was another pivotal moment in the struggle. Aung San Suu Kyi's letter marked the beginning of what turned out to be an eight-year confrontation between the SLORC and The Lady. Or, as a prominent Burmese dissident describes it, "That was the moment when a Volkswagen and a bus went on a collision course that would result in countless human casualties."

Within days, Daw Suu Kyi became a public figure, speaking out for human-rights and a liberal free-market economic system. On August 26, surrounded by her supporters, she stood on the sloping steps of the Shwedagon Pagoda, the most famous symbol of Buddhism in the world, and spoke to a crowd estimated at half a million people. Her message was simple: nonviolence, human-rights, and democracy. It was an emotional speech, especially for those who remembered when her father, General Aung San, stood on the steps of the Shwedagon Pagoda in 1947, and addressed a crowd of thousands on democracy and independence from the British. For them, General Aung San's daughter not only was a poignant reminder of the past, but a living symbol of hope for the future.

On September 18, 1988, any faith that the people had for democratic reform was suddenly smashed when General Saw Maung, the Chief of Staff, announced over the radio that the military had reassumed power and established what would be called the State Law and Order Restoration Council, or SLORC.

For the second time in two months, martial law was imposed throughout the country, and all state institutions were dissolved. The Union of Burma became the Union of Myanmar when the SLORC officially changed the country's name, claiming that *Burma* was a vestige of European colonialism, while *Myanmar*, was a name that evoked pride among the people as it encompassed all the national races throughout the country.

Hundreds of thousands of people took to the streets in protest and in the following days, over 500 were reportedly gunned downed by troops. But when General Saw Maung, as commander-in-chief of the armed forces, saw the scale of the protest, he made a monumental announcement. The SLORC would hold democratic elections in May 1990. What followed would have been incomprehensible anywhere on earth except in Burma under the SLORC.

Despite promising multiparty elections, the military government proceeded to ban all public political gatherings, enforcing severe prison terms for any citizen who disobeyed. Nonetheless, in line with the new multiparty regulations, Aung San Suu Kyi, along with General U Tin U and Colonel U Kyi Maung, founded the National League for Democracy party. The house on University Avenue, already transformed into Daw Khin Kyi's private hospital, became the center for the pro-democracy movement.

Aung San Suu Kyi set out on the campaign trail, traveling around the country, and daring to speak out for democracy and change. That she found the courage to rally crowds in such a dangerous atmosphere only underscores the incredible change that she had made in so short a time from academic, wife, and mother to political leader. "When I first went out campaigning," Daw Suu Kyi explains, "a very very old abbot—well over ninty— gave me two bits of advice. The first was that to get happiness, you have to invest in suffering. The second was that if you want to indulge in honest politics, you've got to be prepared to be reviled and attacked. He was right. I'll tell you something—some of the monks have given me the soundest political advice."

Within days, Daw Suu Kyi was embraced and recognized by the people as the most prominent opposition leader. In a country where people always referred to Ne Win as the "Old Man," or simply as "Number One," Daw Suu Kyi broke all the rules by at-

tacking Ne Win by name. Accusing him of betraying the principles of his colleagues, especially those of her father, Daw Suu Kyi
called on the military to overthrow him, and challenged the
SLORC to transfer its loyalties to the people. "Ne Win is the one
who caused this nation to suffer for twenty-six years," Daw Suu
Kyi told an exuberant crowd. "Ne Win is the one who lowered the
prestige of the armed forces."

Suddenly, the rumors circulating around Burma focused on
Ne Win himself, as people began whispering that the Old Man
still was the sole power behind the SLORC. One Burmese man
who has spent almost his entire life in conflict and opposition to
the military, and who also happens to be related to Ne Win and
knows him well, offers this explanation for the dictator's abrupt
departure, as well as his continuing role during and after the
events of 1988.

"Ne Win wanted to be known as the man who brought
democracy to Burma," the Burmese dissident explains. "In 1988,
when he realized that he had failed, he knew if he didn't resign
he would be thrown out or killed. He created the SLORC because
he believed *wrongly* that the SLORC would never be able to restore law and order. Ne Win also allowed Suu Kyi to remain in
the country and travel around with absolute freedom, whether
she was talking against the government, or advocating democracy. In another example of his convoluted logic, Ne Win *wrongly*
believed that Suu would further splinter the people against the
SLORC so that ultimately Ne Win would be called back to power
to save the nation."

If General Ne Win's plan was to use Aung San Suu Kyi to turn
the people against the SLORC so that he would be called back to
save the nation, not only did the plan fail but it was ultimately
used against him. When Daw Suu Kyi finally decided to become
involved in leading Burma toward democracy, she not only ral-
lied the people against the SLORC, but she encouraged them to
reject anything that had to do with Ne Win and his government.
She also, at the same time, promoted dialogue with the SLORC,
as well as with the military. The ultimate irony was that General

Ne Win had always considered himself to be the legitimate heir of General Aung San. A mere month after his resignation, however, he suddenly discovered that he had a viable challenger in the person of General Aung San's daughter, Aung San Suu Kyi.

As the military increased their pressure on Daw Suu Kyi to renounce her political activities, she reacted by growing even more bold. One incident that has become almost folklore occurred on April 5, 1989, when Suu Kyi and several of her supporters were walking down a road in the Burmese village of Danubyu. According to eyewitnesses, six soldiers jumped out of a jeep, crouched down, and on the orders of a captain, aimed their guns at Daw Suu Kyi, seconds away from firing. In response, Daw Suu Kyi calmly waved away her supporters and continued to walk unperturbed down the road. At the last moment, an officer with the rank of major stopped the countdown. At the time, one of the people with her remarked that perhaps the officer who stopped his men from shooting realized that to turn a martyr into a saint could only further harm an already-tarnished image of the military regime.

Of her actions that day, Daw Suu Kyi says, "It seemed so much simpler to provide a single target than to bring everyone else in."

That modest explanation stems from a philosophy that would serve Daw Suu Kyi well in the years to come. "You should never let your fears prevent you from doing what you know is right," she explains. "Not that you shouldn't be afraid. Fear is normal. But to be inhibited from doing what you know is right is dangerous. You should be able to lead your life in the right way—despite your fears."

On December 27, 1988, nine months after suffering a stroke, Aung San Suu Kyi's mother, Daw Khin Kyi, died peacefully at home. By then, the struggle for human-rights and democracy in Burma was no longer a matter of intermittent demonstrations and scattered violence, countered by sporadic gunfire and random arrests. Throughout the entire country, from the cities to the rural border areas, the people were united in their demand for multiparty democratic rule, even if in some cases the reasons were more self-interest than anti-SLORC.

In Rangoon, events changed on a daily basis and with them the emotions of the people. From one day to the next, hope turned to despair, courage to fear. While the SLORC periodically cleared the streets with gunfire, or broke into houses in the middle of the night to drag people off to jail, they continued to promise that after the elections they would transfer power to the newly installed civilian government. In another example of contradiction, however, while encouraging hundreds of political parties to declare themselves in the upcoming elections, the SLORC also restricted freedom of speech and assembly for members of those parties. Harsh prison sentences without due process of law were handed down on those who disobeyed, especially on members of the National League for Democracy party and supporters of Aung San Suu Kyi.

An Amnesty International report written in 1991 claims that during the months leading up to the elections, hundreds of NLD members ended up in Insein Prison where they were tortured, beaten, and, in a few cases, killed. When it came to general crowd control, the SLORC was an equal opportunity oppressor. The military shot first and asked questions later. According to one Rangoon diplomat, an assault against demonstrators during the 1988 riots occurred in front of the American Embassy, and was nothing more than "an ambush."

"There was no attempt to scatter the crowds," the diplomat recounts, "other than by shooting to kill. And once the people ran, the army followed. Chasing the students, the soldiers fired at random into nearby buildings. Demonstrators were rounded up afterwards, and if they weren't summarily executed, they were forced into service as porters in areas where ethnic insurgents were active."

The general consensus was that the SLORC counted on the hundreds of political parties that emerged just prior to the election to diffuse the vote and cause a split in parliament. When that happened, the government's plan was to step in and take control, declaring that they had "once again saved the country from anarchy and insurrection." In fact, at the time, the head of the SLORC, General Saw Maung, went so far as to predict the outcome of the elections by stating publicly that "the results would be a coalition of many parties that would result in a pre-dominantly military government."

On January 2, 1989, the day of Daw Khin Kyi's funeral, a spirit of unity prevailed throughout Rangoon for the first time in decades. The SLORC announced that all Burmese people would be allowed to gather "freely and without restriction" to attend the "funeral of the widow of Burma's national hero." For many, that gesture by the SLORC was indicative of what the country could be if ever elections would produce a democratic coalition. Tranquility was short-lived, however, when immediately after the ceremonies, the SLORC escalated their use of violence to control the growing anti-government sentiments. Prominent citizens who expressed pro-democracy views were arrested and hauled off to Insein Prison on trumped-up charges.

One example of a random arrest and incarceration without a fair trial happened to "William."

Informed by the SLORC that they had proof that he had engaged in a money-laundering scheme to support dissident groups throughout the country, William was sentenced to six years in solitary confinement in Insein Prison. It would be the first of two sentences handed down by the SLORC that he would be forced to serve.

"The charges were ridiculous," William insists. "The truth is that I had sold my car and gave the money to several students who couldn't pay their tuition. The SLORC took that as an op-portunity to arrest me for instigating violence on the university campus."

William described for me those six years in meticulous detail. His story allowed me to understand what countless other pro-democracy advocates went through back then, and continue to endure today. As for William, not only had he survived the or-deal, but he was able to talk about it calmly, with moments of humor, and admit quite matter-of-factly that he was currently even on speaking terms with several high-ranking SLORC generals. According to William, certain members of the military regime periodically consulted him when they were unsure how to react to statements made by Aung San Suu Kyi, or when they were hesitant about approving or denying requests for visas made by several American politicians. William tells his story.

I lived on a cell block that had fourteen rooms. My cell was eight feet by ten feet and fifteen feet high, with a door that was secured by an iron bar that was four inches thick. I lived with the weather; that is, if it rained, I was wet, if there was scorching sun, I burned, cold winds and I froze. During the monsoon season, the rain would fall laterally through the small window into my cell.

Every day was hell. Each day, I was allowed out of my cell for fifteen minutes to bathe. Prisoners were allowed visits with their families once a month for fifteen minutes, which is how a lot of us survived. Regulations allowed us to receive food and medicine. When I arrived there, I was given two pans about the size of flower pots, one was to urinate, the other to defecate. There was no hygienic paper so often I would tear up a *longyi* for those purposes. I slept on a bamboo mattress with two blankets, one was to cover me and the other I used as a sheet. Sometimes the door was opened once a day and I could stay outside for two to five hours depending on the guard and the general situation in the streets. Twice a day I was fed beans and rice. Every three days I was searched, because paper and writing material were forbidden. Once a guard found a refill from a ballpoint pen and, as a punishment, he denied me food from the outside for three months.

Every day I learned four lines of *Pali* [the language used in the Holy Scriptures]. My daughter photocopied an entire book and the warden agreed to keep it. He would give me one piece of paper written in *Pali* every day and I would write against the wall using my plastic eating utensils. I never knew what I was memorizing. After I was released I went to see a monk who corrected my pronunciation, and told me what the words meant.

I was never tortured but I used to hear others being tortured in the cells near me. Prisoners would get beaten for any small infringement of the rules. Political prisoners were often isolated. Criminals were beaten more regularly.

I survived because I'm a Buddhist and I meditated—that gave me great solace—and because I believe that human beings are resilient and can survive almost anything. Eventually, I learned to sit for hours without moving a muscle or blinking.

When I was released, it was without warning. Since I never had a trial, I never had a specific sentence. One day a guard came into my cell and told me that I would be released if I gave the correct answers to several questions: What did I think of the SLORC? What were my future plans?

What I didn't know at the time was that my release was never contingent on my answering those questions. It had already been decided that I would be released. Those questions were just a matter of form. The reason I was released was because the SLORC wanted to show the world that even a bad person could be forgiven. The SLORC wanted to balance me against Suu Kyi. Then they stopped releasing people for the next two years because they did not get the positive world opinion they believed they would.

As for the questions, they weren't difficult for me to answer since I believe in democracy and the SLORC always claimed to be paving the way toward the goal of democracy. Regarding my future plans, I said that since I had always been good at business, I would return to doing business.

During my imprisonment, I had lost most of my teeth and about forty pounds. The danger for most prisoners after they are released from Insein is that they immediately begin eating rich foods they believe are nourishing. Their bodies, however, are no longer used to that kind of diet so usually after six months, the majority of them die. I've tried to be careful.

On the day I met with William at his house in Rangoon in October 1996, he had just come back from the funeral of a friend who had been released from Insein after serving exactly six months and two days. With a small smile, William told me, "My friend was called Tun Shwe. He died of a heart attack, but of course the SLORC would say that he died from eating rich food."

10

DESPITE A CAMPAIGN to vilify Daw Suu Kyi and harass her supporters, the SLORC eventually realized that those methods only made people more loyal to her and more committed to the quest for democracy. The more Daw Suu Kyi traveled around Burma, speaking out against the SLORC and against General Ne Win, the more people gathered to listen, and the more the military perceived her as the main obstacle to their gaining total political control.

In the days leading up to the annual commemoration of Martyrs' Day, July 19, when the country mourns the assassination of General Aung San and his cabinet, Daw Suu Kyi delivered a speech in which she dared categorically to brand the SLORC liars, charging them with having no intention of ever transferring power to a civilian government, regardless of the outcome of the elections. Exacerbating an already volatile situation, she also announced her intention to lead her own demonstration to pay tribute to her father and his fallen colleagues.

In response, the military took action. Calling out several battalions of troops, the SLORC issued a statement that it was prepared to take "preventative measures to maintain law and order." Aware that the situation was highly incendiary, and fearing a repeat of the bloodshed of the previous year, Aung San Suu Kyi called off the demonstration.

On July 20, 1989, the day after the forty-second anniversary of her father's death, eleven trucks of armed troops rolled down University Avenue, blocking off either egress, as well as preventing anyone from leaving or entering Aung San Suu Kyi's compound. With Suu that day was Win Htein, one of her personal assistants, who remembers what happened.

"Soldiers surrounded the place in the morning," Win Htein begins, "but they didn't take any action until the afternoon. We were just waiting inside the compound. At around 4 P.M. that day, the authorities came in and U Tin U, U Kyi Maung, and others were requested to go outside and leave. But I was to stay. I was the eldest of a group of about forty people who were detained. Some people were released gradually after three months, eight months, two years, three years. I was the only one who was kept in jail for five and a half years."

Also with Daw Suu Kyi on that fateful day were her two sons, Alexander and Kim, then aged sixteen and twelve, who happened to be visiting. Michael Aris was in Scotland, attending the funeral of his own father.

"I thought if they were going to take me to prison," Daw Suu Kyi recalls, "then at least I should have a bag packed with essentials, such as a toothbrush and a change of clothes." She smiles. "After I did that, we all had a nice time just waiting." Another assistant who happened to be with Daw Suu Kyi in the compound that day in July distracted the boys by playing Monopoly with them while they waited for their mother to be arrested.

Several hours after the first appearance of troops, a half dozen soldiers walked into the house, cut the telephone wires, and began searching for documents. While drawers were emptied, files rifled, and closets and cupboards searched, two senior officers arrived and accused Aung San Suu Kyi of being a "dangerous subversive" for planning a rival commemoration of Martyrs' Day. Without being formally charged or allowed to engage a lawyer to defend herself, Aung San Suu Kyi was officially placed under house arrest.

U Kyi Maung, Daw Suu Kyi's close associate, issued the following statement on behalf of the National League for Democracy party. "Aung San Suu Kyi's detention clearly shows that there are absolutely no democratic rights or basic human-rights in Burma under the SLORC." Within days, U Kyi Maung was arrested and taken away to Insein Prison. It was to be the first of two times that he was incarcerated by the SLORC.

The SLORC's justification, when confronted with the fact that Aung San Suu Kyi was detained for six years without any due process of law, is typical of how half-truths and outright lies are the fiber with which their policies are woven. According to one of the legal advisors to the SLORC, Myo Htun Lynn, who had once been a respected barrister-at-law in Burma, it was for The Lady's benefit that she was never charged and put on trial. "Had we ever formally charged Aung San Suu Kyi, it would have been with treason, which automatically carries a death penalty."

Instead of the extreme, therefore, which would have been treason, Daw Suu Kyi was charged with nothing.

"The Lady was never under a state of arrest," Myo Htun Lynn continues, "since she always had the choice of leaving the country and returning to her family."

The SLORC would have the world believe that Aung San Suu Kyi remained a prisoner in her own house for six years by choice.

"She was prepared to do anything to call attention to herself," the legal advisor concludes, "because she had grown bored with her life in England."

Daw Suu Kyi's personal assistant who distracted the boys by playing Monopoly with them was eventually arrested as well, and imprisoned in Insein Prison for three years for her pro-democracy activities. After her release, she gave up politics and started another career in the art world. Currently, she lives with an American journalist who works for an Asian newspaper. She has made a surprising transition from objective reporter to SLORC apologist. The former assistant, although not on particularly good terms with Daw Suu Kyi today, nonetheless remembers how well she and her sons behaved during those tense moments.

"Kim asked his mother if the soldiers were going to take her away," the former assistant begins, "to which Suu replied, 'No darling, I'm going to be locked up in the house.'" According to the former assistant, the boys took the events in their stride. "After all," she continues, "Suu raised the boys to have a British stiff-upper-lip mentality, the same way that she was raised by her own mother."

The well-being of the Aris children, as far as Aung San Suu Kyi felt at the time, was not a potential problem, although she admits her concern for arranging safe passage out of the country for them since they would be leaving unescorted. "My only worry was that my sons got back safely to England, especially if Michael was not allowed to come and get them," Daw Suu Kyi says. As it turned out, Michael Aris was allowed to come to get the children, although the circumstances of his arrival were once again typical of how the SLORC, in their convoluted judgment, managed to transform a straightforward event into a scene from George Orwell's *1984*.

When Michael arrived at Mingaladon Airport in Rangoon, he caused almost as much international concern as his wife's sudden incarceration. As his plane touched down, soldiers, army trucks, and police were all over the tarmac. Whisked away to the rather seedy airport VIP lounge, furnished with formica tables and chairs, plastic plants, and a flickering overhead fluorescent light fixture, Michael was informed of the rules. According to the military officer who had met his plane, he would be allowed to join his family at the compound on University Avenue only if he agreed to the same conditions that applied to his wife, specifically, no contact with any person involved in politics, or anyone belonging to the diplomatic corps, including the British Embassy official who had come to meet him at the airport. Michael agreed and was driven away to see his family.

For the next twenty-one days, the representative from the British Embassy and Michael's family back in England were left wondering what had happened to the Oxford don.

"Obviously, I agreed with the conditions the military set

down," Michael wrote at the time, "since I was able to truthfully say that I had only come to be with the family and saw no difficulty in abiding by those terms. We drove off from the airport to find the house surrounded by troops. The gates were opened and we drove in. I had no idea what to expect."

Michael found his wife in the third day of a hunger strike, having eaten her last meal on July 20, the day she was placed under house arrest. In an effort to protect her colleagues from torture and extreme punishment, her demand was simple. She asked to be transferred to the same prison where they were being held. The authorities denied her request.

For the next twelve days, Daw Suu Kyi accepted only water, until on August 1, a SLORC official came to the house to announce that The Lady's friends and colleagues currently in Insein Prison would not be tortured or harmed and would be allowed an opportunity to plead their cases in a court of law. She accepted the compromise and allowed the doctors assigned to monitor her to put her on an intravenous drip. According to Michael, his wife lost twelve pounds in twelve days. As for her colleagues in jail, some returned, others did not.

From the moment Michael arrived in Rangoon, his transformation began—from husband, father, and Oxford don, to a man who was clearly distraught and frustrated by his apparent inability to secure his wife's release. From the beginning and throughout the entire time that Daw Suu Kyi was confined to her house, Michael was her most ardent defender, a role that was not unusual for any man whose wife and the mother of his children was under house arrest. In fact, Daw Suu Kyi confirms this when she says, "Until I was placed under house arrest, Michael had nothing to do with my political work at all. Of course, after that he did what he could, which was his duty and responsibility as my husband. It was unfortunate since politics is not at all his forte."

Yet there were many people, especially journalists and, above all, the SLORC, who interpreted Michael's involvement in his wife's plight as proof that he had become her official spokesperson. For the regime, it was an excuse to latch onto the fact that Michael Aris was a foreigner, meddling in the affairs of the Burmese government, and by extension, so was his wife. Nonetheless, Michael found himself in a role to which he had never aspired nor dreamed he would be forced to assume. "I was only Suu's defender," Michael claims. "I was not a politician nor am I Burmese. I was literally just her husband, and as her husband I did and said everything I could to get her released."

A quiet academic who treasured his privacy and was known for burying himself in his work, Michael had never imagined that in midlife he would be thrust into the international spotlight and made to cope as a single parent to two adolescent boys. What made Michael's role even more ambiguous was that during the six years that his wife was kept in isolation in her house, he was often forced to speak to the press, if for no other reason than to contradict some of the more fantastic claims the SLORC made. In fact, there were many times when Michael found himself in the unenviable position of pleading his wife's case to a variety of international human-rights groups and even, at times, speaking out for multiparty democracy in an effort to keep the cause alive. Never in all that time, however, did Michael act as a delegate or politician.

A friend of the family explains. "It's very hard to pin it down but Michael Aris could never win in that situation regardless of what he said or did because he was always seen as a protagonist. People interpreted his actions even if there was nothing to analyze."

Despite Michael's reticence in becoming Aung San Suu Kyi's voice, his efforts to make the world aware of the political situation in Burma as well as his wife's personal plight eventually garnered specific international attention. There are some people who insist that Michael was at least partially responsible for his wife drawing the attention of the academy that ultimately awarded her the Nobel Peace Prize in 1991.

During those first few weeks when Daw Suu Kyi was confined to her house, Michael and the boys remained in Rangoon, putting the house in order and making arrangements with the authorities to allow certain medicines and other necessities to be brought in as needed. According to one SLORC official, by allowing Michael to remain near Daw Suu Kyi during those weeks, the government hoped that he would convince her that she had a duty to her family. "We hoped that Mr. Aris would make The Lady see reason," the SLORC official admits, "by persuading her to return to England where she belonged with her husband and children."

What distressed Michael was the fact that their marriage appeared suddenly to be under close scrutiny, not only by the SLORC, but by anybody who decided to write or report on the ongoing situation on University Avenue in Rangoon. Often, nothing of any political significance happened for days and weeks. Creating domestic havoc in the house on University Avenue certainly made media reports more interesting.

When it became clear to the military regime that The Lady had no intention of leaving Burma, even if that meant she would be forced to live without her husband and children, slanderous editorials and articles appeared with regularity in *The New Light of Myanmar*, the highly censored and government-controlled newspaper. The gist of those newspaper pieces speculated on the reasons The Lady had chosen house arrest over her family.

A retired professor at Yangon Institute of Technology, whose current role is to brief foreign journalists on the SLORC's version of history, offered me his opinion on why Aung San Suu Kyi elected to stay in Rangoon when she was given the option to leave.

"Why did she decide to leave her children and her husband?" he asked rhetorically. "I talked to her when she was first married to Mr. Aris and had only one baby and came back during Ne Win's time to lay a wreath at her father's grave. She told me then that she had no intention of ever moving back to Rangoon. Obviously, by the time she was placed under house confinement, there was already trouble in her marriage or she never would have suddenly decided to abandon her husband and two children."

The Deputy Minister of Education, Dr. Khin Maung Nyunt, concurred with that conjecture when he made the following comment during an interview in his office. "Frankly, it is a perverse way of running one's emotional life when the alternative to divorce is house arrest. Why should our country be involved in the domestic troubles of one couple?"

Although Daw Suu Kyi's supporters were often surprised by her stoic manner, they all knew that the decision to sacrifice her family for her country had not been easy. Even Daw Suu Kyi's former assistant, who departed on terms that were somewhat strained, recalls one particularly poignant conversation. "When she would think about her family, she would get tears in her eyes," the woman recalls, "until one day, she simply told me that from now on, she intended to concentrate on her 'new children,' which were all the Burmese people who were fighting for democracy."

There was one particular incident that got a great deal of media attention, and one that the SLORC used in an effort to prove that The Lady's marriage was anything but idyllic.

At a moment during her detention when Daw Suu Kyi had made several crucial demands of the SLORC, Michael was suddenly issued a visa to visit her. At the time, Michael had no idea what the problems were in Rangoon, and Daw Suu Kyi was not told by the regime that they had given her husband permission to come there. "In retrospect," Michael once explained, "it's clear that they [the SLORC] issued me the visa at that particular time either to soften Suu's demands on them, or to improve their own international image."

At the time, Michael was teaching at Harvard University in Cambridge, Massachusetts, in the Department of Sanskrit and Indian Studies. Upon his arrival at the house on University Avenue, Daw Suu Kyi was distraught that the SLORC had apparently used her husband as a pawn in their political games. "Suu asked me to stay in her aunt's house, which was in the compound, until the SLORC agreed with at least one of her demands, which was to keep her informed of any permission for her family to visit."

After several days the SLORC agreed, and Michael simply moved across the compound and into his wife's house during the first of what would be several visits that continued for the remainder of her house arrest. The SLORC's version of that particular event, however, was that The Lady not only constantly refused Michael's phone calls, but when he arrived, slammed the door in his face.

General U Tin U remembers the incident well. "Other members of the NLD were in jail," U Tin U explains. "The last thing Suu wanted was to give the impression that she was not suffering, and that the SLORC would even allow her to see her family whenever she pleased." He adds. "At the time, it was amusing to see Suu's stubbornness when she made Michael go to her aunt's house," U Tin U recalls. "Although it wasn't amusing at all, neither for Michael nor for Suu."

Daw Suu Kyi has always insisted that she never wanted to appear as if she were taking advantage of any lenient treatment by the SLORC, especially when their treatment of her colleagues was much more harsh. "I was in a relatively good position," she explains, "because I had the luxury of not having to worry about my family. They were safe outside the country, unlike many of my colleagues who were in prison inside the country and whose families were left to fend for themselves. For them, it was just one more problem to agonize over while they were in jail."

For a very long time, Michael was silent. When he finally commented on his wife's determination during that difficult period, as well as on the SLORC's persistence in denigrating his marriage, he wrote his version of events in a collection of essays by and about Daw Suu Kyi that he compiled, entitled *Freedom from Fear*. "Very obviously," Michael wrote, "the [SLORC] plan was to break Suu's spirit by separating her from her children in the hope she would accept permanent exile." And, in a subsequent interview, he added, "Anyway, there was never any point in my trying to convince Suu to do anything but what she had decided to do."

As for what she considered to be her reason for confronting the SLORC at every instance, Daw Suu Kyi explains, "The concept of trying to drive someone out of his own country is totally unacceptable to me. Whatever they did to me, I could take. What was more important was what they were doing to the country."

11

IN THE BEGINNING of her six-year detention, Daw Suu Kyi would work in her garden while chatting with the soldiers who guarded her. There were times during her ordeal when she didn't have enough to eat, and as a result her hair fell out and often she was too weak to get out of bed. Other times, she was afraid she had damaged her heart since every time she moved she had palpitations. Her weight fell from a slight 106 pounds to a weakened 90, and she was certain that if she didn't die of heart failure, she would succumb to starvation. Her eyes began to deteriorate as well, and she developed spondylosis, a degenerative condition of the spinal column. Yet through it all, The Lady claims, pointing to her head, "They [the SLORC] never got me here."

According to her, she was inspired by Nelson Mandela and his book, *Long Walk to Freedom*, as well as by Ghandi and his philosophy of passive resistance. What gave her strength throughout her ordeal was the realization that many of her friends and colleagues involved with her in the quest for democracy were confined to the notorious Insein Prison where they endured torture, sleep deprivation, and lack of food. Some never lived to tell their tales.

In the first few weeks of detention, before the rains came, while Daw Suu Kyi worked in her garden, talking with her guards, they touched on every subject except politics. "On the day they placed me under house arrest," Daw Suu Kyi recalls, "the garden was quite beautiful. There were lots of white madonna lilies, fields and fields of them, and frangipani and fragrant yellow jasmine and gardenias, all highly scented flowers. There was also a flower from South America that changes color as it matures, called Yesterday, Today, and Tomorrow."

The most interesting discussions, she claims, were with one of her liaison officers, a colonel in rank, whom she was certain reported everything she said back to his superiors. "Even though he always tried to put forth his point of view when it came to Burmese history and politics," Daw Suu Kyi says, "I thoroughly enjoyed our talks."

After a while, Suu was obliged to let the garden grow wild as she had neither the money nor the strength to keep it pruned. Eventually, it grew so wild that it resembled a tropical jungle. The joke going around Rangoon back then was that the military regime was so afraid of The Lady that they hoped the tropical vines and luxuriant flowering bushes would eventually smother the house and at last silence its occupant.

After she was released and could mobilize people to help, she discovered the garden was filled with snakes.

The day that Aung San Suu Kyi was put under house arrest, the SLORC put up signs saying No U-Turn and No Slowing Down, written in Burmese and English, that were displayed prominently along the gate. Making every effort to turn The Lady into a nonperson, the police removed the number from her house. Even the guards were invisible to the casual observer, although fifteen armed soldiers were on duty at all times, well hidden within the compound. Twice a day, at the end of each eight-hour shift, they would be bused in and out in an army van. Eventually, over the years, the SLORC came to understand that it was necessary to change the guards frequently for fear they would succumb to The Lady's charm, personality, and, of course, be touched by her relationship to their national hero, General Aung San.

The SLORC's feelings about Aung San Suu Kyi have always been ambiguous. When it comes to her political activities, The

Lady is treated harshly by the regime. When it comes to her relationship with General Aung San, the SLORC allows her to assume the guardianship of her father's legacy, and to function as the keeper of his memory, honor, and name. The latter was made especially evident during the time that Daw Suu Kyi was under house arrest. The soldiers who guarded her never forgot that the *Tatmadaw*, or Burmese Army, had been her father's creation. One of the most interesting dimensions to Aung San Suu Kyi, and one of the primary reasons why she has found a permanent place in the hearts and minds of the Burmese peoples, is what is often called the "Aung San factor."

Indeed, most citizens believe that Daw Suu Kyi can rightfully use her father's memory to call attention back to 1948 and to draw on political history and traditions that touch a collective and familiar chord in the hearts of all the people.

* * *

At four o'clock one morning during my first trip to Rangoon, there was a knock on my door. Terrified that the moment had finally come when I would be thrown out of the country or taken away to jail, I was relieved to see a foreign diplomat, dressed in bermuda shorts and a T-shirt. He told me that he had arranged an appointment for me to talk to several of the soldiers who had guarded Suu Kyi. Throwing on clothes, I quickly ran downstairs, and got into the waiting car. Approximately thirty-five minutes later, we stopped in front of a remote, run-down building several kilometers outside Rangoon.

The building appeared to be abandoned except for one floor where several soldiers were waiting. Apparently, each one had spent four months on duty at Daw Suu Kyi's compound when she was under house arrest. Each offered me his impression of The Lady.

"Often, Aung San Suu Kyi was arrogant," one soldier claimed, "but just as quickly she could be friendly."

I asked another how he felt guarding the daughter of a national hero.

"At first, I felt I was a soldier who had a duty to the army, but at the same time, it was sad for me to guard the daughter of General Aung San, especially since I came to believe that she only wanted the best for the Burmese people."

Of another I asked if he felt himself treating her more respectfully than he would another prisoner.

"I felt privileged to be in her presence," the soldier replied, "although I understood that I was not supposed to talk to her except when she began a conversation. My superior officer ordered all of us who were there with Aung San Suu Kyi to listen for specific names or places that would yield other enemies of the SLORC. But mostly when she talked to me, it was about her garden."

I asked about her mental state during those months when he guarded her.

"The one thing I remember best about her was how she seemed completely calm and at peace with the situation. I never saw her upset or frightened. There was a great dignity about her and the way she responded to everything that happened and, although I can't mention specific incidents for obvious reasons, I can say that her biggest concern was always about her friends who were in prison."

*　　*　　*

From the very beginning of Daw Suu Kyi's house arrest, the SLORC agreed that Michael could send his wife books, letters, and personal provisions through the British diplomatic pouch. Since Suu refused to accept anything from the SLORC, the regime was afraid that unless they allowed certain supplies to reach her, she would get sick or even die. But in another example of the military's duplicitous tactics, they leaked what they called "The Lady's privileged foreign connection" to the local state-sponsored press in an effort to taint Daw Suu Kyi in the minds of the Burmese people. Offering proof of their claims, the SLORC confiscated several packages, and photographed their contents, showing among other items that had been included, several lipsticks and a Jane Fonda exercise tape. Immediately, Daw Suu Kyi put a stop to the packages. Still, she refused to accept anything from the SLORC, including food and even electricity.

According to a SLORC intelligence officer, there was a point in The Lady's confinement when there was nothing in the house to eat except one container of rice. Soon after that, rumors spread all the way to Oxford that she had gone on another hunger strike, and that her weight had dropped significantly. "I just want to make something very clear," Daw Suu Kyi says now. "Except for my one and only hunger strike at the very beginning of my detention, there was never any other. The rumors began because for a while, there was literally no food in the house, and actually no money to buy any food."

Eventually Daw Suu Kyi came to an arrangement with the SLORC where in return for services and food, she sold them some of the better pieces of her furniture. As it turned out, the government, without her knowledge, stored the furniture in a warehouse with the intention of giving it back to her at some point. (After her release, Daw Suu Kyi refused the SLORC's offers to return the furniture, and instead arranged to pay for the pieces as money was available.)

But even after Daw Suu Kyi began selling off pieces of furniture to the SLORC, there was still barely enough money to buy food and personal necessities to carry her for any length of time. She sustained her body and mind by a rigorous schedule that included exercise, meditation, reading, playing the piano before it was irreparably out of tune, and listening to the radio. It was the meditation, however, that she claims did her the most good. It taught her patience, she says, an accomplishment for someone who always had a rather short temper. Practicing insight meditation, Daw Suu Kyi perfected the technique of concentrating on her breathing until she went into a kind of self-hypnotic trance. "Meditating develops a sense of awareness and that means better control of your emotions," Daw Suu Kyi explains. "By nature,

I'm a disciplined person so it became very easy for me to develop a stringent routine."

Up at four every morning, she would tidy up before sitting at the foot of her bed in a half lotus position to meditate for one hour. At 5:30 she tuned in to the radio for two hours, beginning with the *BBC World Service News* in English, followed by the *BBC Burmese Services*, the Voice of America and the DVB broadcast from Norway.

When she was released, she told everyone that despite her isolation, she felt in touch with the world, something that made her acutely aware of what her colleagues were going through in Insein Prison. "I was living in a more or less comfortable house," she explained, "rather dilapidated but all right. I slept on clean sheets and I had books and the radio. But a lot of my colleagues were not in that position. They went through a terrible time. And I thought that if they can take it, so can I."

When the radio finished for the morning, Daw Suu Kyi would do aerobics and then exercise on a Nordic Track that her husband had brought on one of his visits. After she bathed and dressed, she would usually read something before breakfast, either a religious work or a political treatise. Breakfast would consist of fruit, tea, and milk, hardly any bread since it was expensive, as were eggs, although she allowed herself one hard-boiled egg on the weekends. At lunchtime, Suu Kyi would once again tune in to the *BBC World Service*.

During the weekday afternoons, she read politics, economics, and philosophy, and on weekends she took time to read more for her own pleasure—books that included biographies of political dissidents such as Nehru, Sharansky, and Sakharov, or books on such inspirational figures as Mother Theresa. In the evening, before going to bed, she would end her day with the *BBC Burmese Services*. What also gave her strength, Daw Suu Kyi admits, was the many times that she looked at her father's picture that hangs high on a wall in her living room, and thought, "Well now, it's just you and me—but we'll make it."

According to Daw Suu Kyi, throughout those six years she

would dream of her husband and children, although she refused to allow herself the luxury of dwelling on them. She was able to cope with the separation the way most political prisoners have done throughout the ages. "I simply stopped agonizing over my family because there was nothing I could do about the situation; I couldn't change things so I learned to control my thoughts."

As far as she was concerned, there was never any doubt that her marriage would survive the separation, although she is quick to add that her marriage hadn't been a conventional marriage for years. "It is painful for any parent not to see his or her own children," Daw Suu Kyi says, "but I think one worries more about children than a spouse because you always expect adults to be able to cope better. My sons did not cope too badly although it was a strain for them."

Recently, Michael confirmed his wife's feelings when he said, "I am a one-woman man. There was never any doubt that Suu felt the same way."

What is curious is that throughout the entire time that Daw Suu Kyi has been leading the pro-democracy movement, and the SLORC has been vilifying her in every conceivable way, never has there been any rumor about her fidelity, nor for that matter, about Michael's.

During the years when she was incarcerated, Daw Suu Kyi recalls that she would concentrate on details in an effort not to focus on time. "My days were organized down to the last minute," she says. Despite her resolve to account for every minute of her time, there often were unexpected problems she had to contend with, such as a leaky roof, which had her running up and down the stairs, positioning buckets to catch the water.

For the first few years of her confinement, her sons lived with their father in Oxford. Although they were allowed sporadic visits with their mother, eventually all contact between them was banned. "I didn't see my children together," Daw Suu Kyi relates. "My elder son came to visit first, you see. He was fifteen when I had last seen him, and he had already taken on his adolescent shape, so when I saw him after all that time, there was not much difference. My younger son, however, was only eleven when I had last seen him, and he was still a little boy. When I finally saw him again, he had changed completely, so much that I don't know if I would have recognized him on the street. I'm not sure I would have known he was my son."

According to sources close to the family in England, Alexander, a serious and intense young man, suffered deeply and silently from his mother's plight. For several of those years, Michael went to Harvard University to teach in the Department of Sanskrit and Indian Studies. It was important that Kim, the younger boy, have as much continuity in his life as possible, which meant that it would be best if he remained in England with his friends, attending the same school. As a result, Kim lived with various members of the family for a period of time, including his aunt and uncle, Marie-Laure and Anthony Aris. "Alexander was always very intense and introverted," Marie-Laure Aris says. "Kim, on the other hand, was always a more outgoing child, certainly more westernized. Typically, while Alexander was usually reading or studying, Kim was playing his guitar."

Even when it came to Daw Suu Kyi's children, it was not beneath the SLORC to print slanderous and hurtful editorials in the state-run newspaper. Periodically references would be made to Alexander's "precarious mental state," and Kim's "decadent western style and long hair." But more damaging were the SLORC's frequent accusations that while the Aris children enjoyed the privilege of elite educations in prestigious foreign schools, Aung San Suu Kyi was intent on persuading the world not to invest money in Burma—a position that, the regime claimed, ultimately harmed the Burmese people, especially the children.

From the moment that I arrived in Rangoon in October 1996, and listened to the conditions the SLORC proposed concerning my research and interviews, the problem was obvious. Everyone whom I would be meeting and interviewing under government auspices would express only the SLORC's point of view. At one point, the regime arranged for me to meet with a professional group of women—mostly academics—who, according to the regime, "would tell me honestly what they thought of Aung San Suu Kyi."

In turn, each woman offered her opinion concerning what they called Aung San Suu Kyi's "contradictory" attitude or "double standards" when it came to Burma and the rest of the world. The women's main complaint was that Daw Suu Kyi was encouraging sanctions on Myanmar that deprived students of books and other learning facilities and tools, while her own children were educated at foreign private schools and universities. At the end of the meeting, the following statement was read by one of the women:

> We, the delegation of Myanmar school teachers, went on a study tour of Japan to observe and learn about the educational system and methods employed there. In the course of this study tour, we received information that although Japan had previously decided to assist Myanmar by building 500 elementary school premises made of brick and corrugated iron roofing, Japan began to have doubts about this program because Daw Aung San Suu Kyi had called on foreign countries not to render any kind of aid or assistance to Myanmar. We heard that finally Japan decided not to give the intended 500 schools. But for us, schoolteachers who are trying to educate the children of Myanmar for their future development and success in life, it is an irreparable loss and we are deeply saddened by it.

Several days later, the same woman who had read me that statement in the presence of the others was waiting for me in front of my guest house. She greeted me with the following statement. "That material that was meant for those 500 schools in Myanmar," she said, "ended up in Vietnam." I thanked her for telling me, and waited. "I'm ashamed," she finally said, tears welling in her eyes. "Some day you'll understand. But you see, I couldn't be sure about the others. . . ."

12

IN MAY 1990, the SLORC kept the only promise it had ever made when it actually held national elections. Yet, in another effort to marginalize Aung San Suu Kyi, the generals promptly announced that as a consequence of her current status under house detention, she was ineligible to run for public office. The removal of Daw Suu Kyi's name from the official ballot did nothing to diminish her influence or her impact on the voting public. The majority of people assumed that any candidate belonging to the pro-democracy party on the ballot was only a temporary stand-in until The Lady was liberated.

When the votes were counted in what was deemed by international observers to be a fair election, Daw Suu Kyi's National League for Democracy party had garnered more than 59.7 percent of the vote. In analyzing the results, Kei Nemoto, a professor at Tokyo University of Foreign Studies, explains, "The results of the elections were staggering as they concerned opposition to the SLORC. The National League for Democracy got 392 seats out of a total of 485 that were available, or more than 80 percent of the entire parliament. And, if the elected politicians from other pro-democracy parties as well as small ethnic groups and independents are counted, the anti-SLORC vote increases to nearly 98 percent."

There were several scholars and other Burma experts who in-

terpreted the fact that the SLORC kept their promise to hold
elections as a sign that the military eventually intended to step
down. After the results were made public, and the National
League for Democracy party won the majority of the vote, those
same scholars and Burma experts were even more optimistic, certain that the SLORC would finally be forced to negotiate some
kind of a compromise with Aung San Suu Kyi. In fact, immediately after the election results, in an effort to encourage some
kind of compromise with the military, Daw Suu Kyi sent the following message to the SLORC:

"I have always said that the military is an honourable profession because it is the best way to protect the interests of the people as well as of the country. . . . We all have a special role to play.
I don't think just one single group has a special role to play in
the nation. Each group has its own value, just as each person has
his own value as a human being in the world."

In September 1990, after the victory of U Kyi Maung's party
in the elections, and after having been released from Insein
Prison, he was arrested again. On that occasion, he was tried by
a military tribunal, and sentenced to twenty years in Insein
Prison. In an act of amnesty, however, he was subsequently released five years later, in March 1995.

Faced with the prospect of being ousted from power, the
SLORC not only ignored the results of the elections, but claimed
that the elections had *not* been held to choose political leaders,
but rather to elect representatives to a National Convention that
would draft the country's third constitution.

The Deputy Minister of Education, Dr. Khin Maung Nyunt,
who also serves as a SLORC-appointed member of the Central
Executive Committee, met with me at his office at Yangon University. "Whatever the perception of the people when they voted,"
Dr. Khin Maung Nyunt explained, "the government had to follow the legality of the system, and the perception may be different from the letter of the law. SLORC was going according
to the letter of the law. For example, recently in Belgium during
the pedophile case, the judge was removed. Why? Because it was

obvious that he was in favor of the children who had been sexually abused and murdered, instead of showing impartiality. So the state took away his power. It was much the same during our elections here, I mean it was the difference between the perception and the letter of the law. For the purpose of eventually handing over power, it was obvious that the country needed a new constitution."

Curiously, the SLORC's excuse that the 1990 elections were to choose representatives to write a new constitution has its basis in Burmese history. As Aung San Suu Kyi explains, "The SLORC has consistently made reference to the fact that because of the ethnic groups who were in the process at the time of being lured back into the 'legal fold,' the 1974 constitution was no longer fair or applicable since it did not include or provide for those national races to share in the process of governing."

As for the millions of Burmese who went to the polls in good faith, believing that they were voting for a new government, the SLORC's sudden switch as to the purpose of the exercise is a perfect twist to the fairy tale "The Emperor's New Clothes." In the fairy tale, while millions of people see with their own eyes that the Emperor is naked, only one brave soul dares to say it out loud. In the case of the 1990 elections, while millions of Burmese knew that the SLORC had created a retroactive fairy tale as to why they had cast their votes, only Aung San Suu Kyi was brave enough to state it publicly.

Beginning with the minions of the SLORC who also serve as minders for foreign visitors, and ending with high-ranking members of the SLORC itself, every response to my questions about the purpose of the elections was the same. "Logically speaking," Noreen, my minder, explained patiently, "without a constitution there cannot be a government. It is the SLORC's priority to have a constitution that applies to the situation in our country today and now we are drafting one."

From the Burmese Ambassador to France came the following comment, "This election was held so that a constitution could be drafted. The NLD is too much in a hurry. From the perspective of the military government, there is still a lot of preparation to be done, and the military government will eventually hand over power but only when we have a strong foundation."

Asked whether the SLORC had perhaps been unprepared for the results of the elections, or had miscalculated the extent to which the people were dissatisfied, General David Abel, the Minister for National Planning and Economic Development, offered the following opinion:

"The truth is that the country was not ready for elections in 1990 although I wouldn't say that the government made a mistake. Don't forget they had promised the people elections and it was supposed to be a fair election. But yes, it was premature. Perhaps if the last government had not made that premature move, the answer would be that the situation would be different today. In reality, however, even under present conditions, it probably would not be any different since we would have to allow the people what they wanted because of pressure from the outside."

Colonel Hla Min, my contact with the SLORC and a close advisor to General Khin Nyunt, addressed the "misunderstanding" that forty-five million Burmese apparently shared concerning the purpose of the elections.

"When the elections were held," Colonel Hla Min explained, "there were people who really understood politics and seriously cast their votes, but there were many other people who cast their ballots based on their dislike for the previous socialist government [Ne Win's government]. They voted for whoever was competing against the army, regardless of what any of those opposition parties stood for. The military government since 1988 has tried to make the country stable and united. It would have been very difficult for the government to immediately hand over power after the elections because that fragile stability would have been broken. The outside world must understand that for us, in our country, stability and peace are more important than democracy or human-rights. If we wanted only to promote democracy and human-rights, it would destabilize our country. And then who suffers? The outside world will not suffer but we will suffer here in Myanmar."

As it turned out, Colonel Hla Min was certainly correct about one thing. After the SLORC refused to honor the results of the 1990 elections and instead, forced the people to believe in yet another fairy tale called the National Convention, the outside world is certainly suffering less than the people in Myanmar.

* * *

After they denied the elections, the SLORC took yet another step to guarantee that Aung San Suu Kyi could never hold public office. Citing the two previous constitutions, one written in 1947 in the time of her father, General Aung San, and the other in 1974 during Ne Win's regime, the SLORC stated that a clause already existed that precluded anyone married to a foreigner, or having spent more than twenty years out of the country, from ever becoming president.

According to General Khin Nyunt, the clause, Section 10-E, had been written into the 1947 constitution by General Aung San. "When her [Aung San Suu Kyi's] name was proposed in the very beginning," General Khin Nyunt explains, "any other party could contest the nomination. In fact, it was challenged by another party, the case was taken to court, and the court rejected the nomination."

According to the National League for Democracy, it was not General Aung San at all, but the SLORC that added that exclusionary clause immediately before the elections in 1990.

"It always seemed ridiculous," Daw Suu Kyi commented, "that the government would rewrite a clause in the constitution to apply just to one specific individual."

There is no doubt, however, that Daw Suu Kyi was aware of the country's prejudice toward Burmese women who married foreigners. In 1916, long before her father gained national prominence, and years before the 1947 constitution was written, the Young Men's Buddhist Association of Burma passed a resolution against foreign intermarriage. According to Daw Suu Kyi, at the time that she married Michael Aris, although aware of the difficulties in marrying a foreigner, politics were the furthest thing from her mind.

In 1989, according to U Kyi Maung, before Suu Kyi was put under house arrest, she and Michael discussed the possibility of divorce. "It was a discussion," Michael Aris explained recently, "that was only meant as a way to get around that SLORC law. But in the end we decided it wasn't worth it since the SLORC would only think up another excuse."

Regardless of Daw Suu Kyi's marital status, William, the prominent anti-SLORC dissident, is convinced that she will never become president of the country. Furthermore, William is also certain that the election results were not indicative of the people's desire for democracy.

While William was in solitary confinement in Insein Prison, he wrote a congratulatory letter to Daw Suu Kyi's colleague, U Kyi Maung, cautioning him about the results. "It was a two-page letter," William explains, "telling him that the NLD got all those votes not because of the party but because the people were dissatisfied. I suggested that instead of demanding anything from the SLORC, the NLD should leave the responsibility in the hands of the SLORC for handing over the government. I advised Kyi Maung to send a representative to the SLORC to try to negotiate a solution. It was an error to demand the formation of a government right away. The SLORC needed time, and the people needed to understand what the NLD was about. In the beginning, the people accepted Suu Kyi because of her name. In reality, the people needed to understand what Suu Kyi stood for."

Immediately after the elections, outside observers—who did not understand the psychology of the Burmese people or the history of the country as well as William or others who had lived there for their entire lives understood it—came to the conclusion that the Burmese Army had rights, the minorities had rights, and the NLD had rights.

By contrast, the SLORC continued—in a policy begun in 1989—to broker peace accords with armed ethnic groups that had been fighting with the central Burmese government for decades. Throughout Rangoon, billboards appeared on which were written the following SLORC slogan.

Our Three Main National Causes
Non-disintegration of the Union—Our Cause!
Non-disintegration of National Sovereignty—Our Cause!
Consolidation of National Sovereignty—Our Cause!

This created an ambiguous picture, for while the first peace in decades came to many long war-torn areas of the country, the political deadlock over the issue of democracy remained in the cities.

The sixteen minority forces who agreed to come back into the "legal fold" did so on the condition that the SLORC would help build up the rural areas where they lived. The SLORC promised to provide a modern infrastructure that would enable those sixteen ethnic groups to transport their crops to city ports where they could be shipped internationally. But in order for the SLORC to keep that promise, which was supposedly the basis for a "crop substitution" program whereby some of the ethnic groups would stop producing opium and begin producing legally acceptable crops, foreign investment was desperately needed. What the SLORC never considered, however, was that any international aid to achieve those goals would be pre-conditioned on Daw Suu Kyi's release from house arrest. Further, without approval of the international community, and without the sanction of the United Nations human-rights commission as well as of other international human-rights groups, the Burmese military regime would find itself without adequate funding to be able to keep those promises.

If the SLORC was forced to break promises made to the ethnic minorities, there is no doubt that there would be an immediate resumption of border clashes and fighting between the government and the minority groups. When that happened, which it surely would, the entire constitutional process that the SLORC claimed was imperative in order to benefit all the "Myanmar people" would be proven to be exactly what it was—a sham.

If the excuse to write a new constitution was suddenly deemed fraudulent, the SLORC would never be able to justify to the world why they nullified the elections.

In 1988, had General Ne Win stepped down because he believed the country was ready for multiparty democracy, a new constitution would have been imperative.

In 1990, had the SLORC honored the multiparty elections, drafting a new constitution would have been a logical first step for the new democratic government.

In either case, had the reasons given by Ne Win and the SLORC been truthful and sincere, Burma would have clearly needed a new constitution to allow for the country's transition from a one-party socialist system to a multiparty democracy.

As the situation stands today, however, with the SLORC in power and the elections nullified, writing a new constitution is an excuse for the SLORC to maintain control. As U Kyi Maung insists, "Drafting a constitution is nothing more than a way to buy time so the SLORC doesn't have to relinquish power."

Daw Suu Kyi agrees, and she adds, "Nothing has changed in Burma since Ne Win resigned except the cast of characters."

David Young, who sits at the Burma Desk at the United States Department of State, says, "Whenever a country or a terrorist group has a political crisis, the group simply changes its name to make the world believe its politics has changed. It's an old trick. The names and faces change, but policy remains the same, and that's exactly what happened in Burma after Ne Win stepped down and the SLORC took over."

In fact, the SLORC even claims that there have been changes within their own government since "a new and younger generation of generals took over in 1992," after General Saw Maung was replaced for "health reasons" by General Khin Nyunt.

"It should be noted," General Khin Nyunt says, "that there is no one individual military dictator ruling Myanmar as there was in the past. Now, there is a determined effort on the part of the government to bring about change in the country."

* * *

On my first visit to Burma, I conducted a three-hour interview with General Khin Nyunt, the most powerful man in the

SLORC. According to General Khin Nyunt, Ne Win resigned, sacrificing his own political career, to save the nation.

"In fact," General Khin Nyunt explained, "contrary to opinion, it was not the army that harmed the people, but rather the army that stepped in and imposed martial law in order to save the people."

The SLORC's version of the events of 1988 is disputed by the majority of Burmese, as well as by groups outside the country. According to U Sein Win, the National League for Democracy's Prime Minister-in-exile who resides in Washington, D.C., and who also happens to be Daw Suu Kyi's cousin, it was the military that instigated the violence. "The army was just waiting for anarchy as an excuse to take over and bring the country to order," Sein Win explains. "In reality, the anarchy was staged by SLORC people who opened up stores and warehouses and started looting. The people just followed."

During our discussion of the events in 1988 and the reason for General Ne Win's sudden departure, General Khin Nyunt suggested that I watch a certain video that was filmed by the government while the violence was actually taking place in the streets.

According to General Khin Nyunt, only after I had seen for myself would I understand that the brutality that took place was perpetrated by civilians at the instigation of the communists.

One portion of the tape shows a clandestine meeting of several Burmese men, described by the SLORC as "well-known Burmese communists," allegedly plotting to overthrow the government by causing fear, violence, and general chaos throughout the country. Unfortunately, the audio portion of the tape was in Burmese and the translation was done by several of General Khin Nyunt's aides, which meant that I had no way of knowing what those "well-known Burmese communists" were plotting, if they were plotting anything at all.

The most disturbing portion of the video, however, was of a group of men and women standing in front of a jail. As a French cameraman records the scene, questioning the apparent leader of the group in heavily accented English, eliciting responses that describe the event that is about to take place, the crowd breaks into the jail and drags out several prisoners who claim they have been incarcerated for petty theft. As the camera rolls, and the voice of the cameraman drones on over the fray, one haggard female prisoner pleads for her life, denying the charges hurled at her by the crowd that she is a cohort and friend of General Ne Win's daughter, Sanda. To no avail. The last image is of the terrified woman being pulled toward the middle of the street where she is repeatedly stabbed by several frenzied members of the crowd. The grand finale to the butchery is a horrific scene in which several young men hold the woman down while another saws off her head with an obviously dull knife.

Present during the screening of that video was Senior General Than Shwe, Chairman of the SLORC, who made the following comment. "When the SLORC first assumed responsibility in 1988 the situation was unimaginable. The country was on the verge of chaos and anarchy. At the time, the army was also very aware of the country's geopolitical situation, since our neighbors—India and China—are two of the most populous nations in the world."

Elaborating on General Than Shwe's version of events, General Khin Nyunt added, "At the time that General Ne Win made his resignation speech, he proposed that the people should vote for a revision of the constitution and this vote should be in a multiparty election. The participants went into a room to vote and when they came out, they announced that they still wanted a one-party system. I happen to know that while *in camera* the army and the defense people argued with Ne Win because they did not want him to resign. Despite their wishes, General Ne Win was determined to resign so that the country could have multiparty elections, which would bring democracy to Myanmar."

According to those SLORC generals who claimed to have been in the audience that day, General Ne Win ended his speech

by saying, "I have failed to bring the country up to a level of prosperity with the Burmese Way to Socialism."

General David Abel, the Anglo-Burmese Minister for National Planning and Economic Development, was not only in the
room during the screening, but, according to him, he was also in
the audience on the day that General Ne Win gave his resignation speech. In response to accusations that General Ne Win
never really resigned, but rather was, and continues to be even
today, the power behind the SLORC, General Abel affirms that
Ne Win was always consistent concerning his decision to step
down.

"What I have done," General Ne Win allegedly told the audience that day, "I have done with sincere motivation. But I failed.
So you don't need to consult me. Don't come to visit me, it's up
to you now." General David Abel goes on to explain, "General Ne
Win understood that his system had failed and that the people
wanted a multiparty democracy. From that day on, he turned his
back on politics, even though on several occasions we tried to
consult him."

Ask the SLORC today, and they will say that 1988 was no
different from the previous fifty years of Burmese history when
the military stepped in to save the country from anarchy and
insurrection.

Colonel U Kyi Maung, Daw Suu Kyi's colleague and one of
the founders of the National League for Democracy party, explains, "When the democracy protests first started in 1988, even
the people who opposed Ne Win didn't trust the democratic
politicians who came forward. They remembered back to 1948
when quasi-democratic governments were fighting amongst
themselves. In fact, many people remembered that, as recently as
1962, the army, under the command of General Ne Win, was
brought in to take power and save the country from internal
fighting."

According to ex-General U Tin U, Ne Win is still the power
behind the scenes today. "Ne Win wanted to show the international community that he wasn't the one creating all the

problems," U Tin U explains. "He only gave up his position because he knew that he had the loyalty of the army and could still pull the strings. As for the current situation, Ne Win is still in charge since General Khin Nyunt is his protege and handpicked successor."

A high-ranking officer, Colonel Kyaw Thein, known also as "The Poppyman" because of his position of overseeing the eradication of poppy and opium throughout the country, was also present when General Ne Win retired. He maintains that the concept of the army as the savior of the country, and especially as the single force to maintain unity within the country, has never changed. "We have always had our own traditions that have not changed very much since the army was founded," Colonel Kyaw Thein begins, "and whenever the army did change, it was only a result of who happened to be in control. From the beginning, our first objective was the liberation of our country from British colonialists in 1948. But as soon as we regained our independence, armed insurgence groups rose up against the government and the country was in chaos, with various groups ruling different areas. Only Yangon remained under the government administration. What happened was that the army had to defend not only the sovereignty of the nation and the existence of the government, but it had to keep the nation united and defend it from outside enemies."

A further explanation of the ambiguous relationship between the Burmese people and the military, seen as both savior and oppressor, is offered by one western analyst. "When you see Suu Kyi sitting next to ex-General Tin U and ex-Colonel Kyi Maung, you begin to understand that the perception that the military are all bad guys is completely wrong. The military has played, and undoubtedly will continue to play, a strong role in Burmese politics, even if there is ever a democratic Burma."

General Khin Nyunt, however, puts it even more simply when he states, "The fate of one person was far less important than the fate of 45 million Burmese."

General Than Shwe, the current chairman of the SLORC,

during an interview I conducted with him in October 1996, attempted to justify the government's decision at the time. "The sole goal of the SLORC was to prevent more bloodshed."

Still, to this day, Burmese diplomats are fond of telling their counterparts on the regional cocktail circuit that, "Without the *Tatmadaw* [armed forces] our country would have been the Yugoslavia of Asia."

13

IN 1991, while Aung San Suu Kyi was still under house arrest, *Freedom from Fear*, a collection of essays by and about her and edited by her husband, Michael Aris, was published by Viking Penguin in England. According to Daw Suu Kyi, it was only then that she learned that some of her personal letters to her husband had been included in the text. "I was upset," she admits, "because I believed private letters should remain private." But she was also realistic. For several years when she under house arrest, she lived largely on the proceeds of the book—yet another contradictory and illogical action on the part of the SLORC.

Why did the military government allow Daw Suu Kyi to deposit royalties from *Freedom from Fear* in a Rangoon bank, and to draw upon the money to pay for her daily living expenses? After all, the book was a tribute to The Lady, and a harsh critique of the SLORC.

At the time, some interpreted the SLORC's decision as a sign that they were weakening their position when it came to negotiating with the pro-democracy movement. But although the regime allowed Daw Suu Kyi to use the money from the book to maintain herself, they also renewed her confinement every six months until the months became years.

"Actually," Daw Suu Kyi explains, "I should have been released three years earlier but the SLORC changed the law. Then,

I should have been released a year before I was, and once again the SLORC changed the interpretation of the law. To have held me longer than they did means that they would have had to change the law again. But I don't believe they released me when they did because of the law. I think they eventually let me go because they felt confident enough that international pressure wouldn't affect their international business ventures."

In 1991, this once obscure Burmese woman, when she had been living in exile for more than two decades and had been under house arrest for three years, was awarded the Nobel Peace Prize. She says she learned that she had won on the radio. "I was very grateful. I felt tremendous humility and gratitude."

There was no better way for the pro-democracy movement in Burma to make the world aware of the political repression throughout the country than for Aung San Suu Kyi to have won the Nobel Peace Prize. Yet, there were many people, especially within Daw Suu Kyi's inner circle, who feared that winning the prize would make it even more difficult for Daw Suu Kyi and the SLORC to come to any compromise. As the eighth woman in history to win the peace prize, and the first to receive it while in captivity, Daw Suu Kyi became the focus of a variety of human-rights groups throughout the world, as well as the United States Department of State under the Clinton administration—which suddenly put the pro-democracy movement in Burma high on its international agenda. When Daw Suu Kyi claims that she felt the responsibility that the prize entailed, it is an understatement.

According to her colleagues in the NLD in Burma, Aung San Suu Kyi suddenly became fearful that she would fail the many people throughout the world who were counting on her to achieve such difficult goals.

As for the SLORC's reaction, according to Colonel Hla Min, the government had no intention of letting the Nobel Peace Prize influence how they intended to run the country. "We respect the integrity of other nations," Colonel Hla Min told me, "and we expect that certain foreign powers will respect our national goals as well. International awards or prizes should have no influence on the internal affairs of any country."

One of the rumors that the SLORC began spreading after Aung San Suu Kyi won the Nobel Prize was that she was less a prisoner of their regime than she was a prisoner of the Swedish Academy that had honored her. Colonel Hla Min repeated this sentiment when he observed, "After The Lady won, even if she wanted to leave and join her family in England, she was suddenly trapped in a situation of her own making." But, according to several members of the NLD, Daw Suu Kyi was less a prisoner of the Nobel Peace Prize than she was a hostage of the media. The eyes of the world were upon her. "Like it or not, she couldn't make a mistake," one pro-democracy colleague claimed. "From one minute to the next, Suu went from being our spokesperson and leader of the NLD, to becoming the property of every liberal movement and human-rights organization throughout the world."

And the rumors continued, some frivolous, others serious. Even Daw Suu Kyi's appearance provoked comment after she won the Nobel Peace Prize, which was not surprising considering the blatant visual difference between The Lady and the SLORC.

On one side of the struggle was a graceful and exotic Asian woman wearing a *longyi* and cotton shirt fitted tightly against her slim frame, with a sprig of yellow flowers woven around a chignon at the nape of her neck, petals falling on her shoulders at the end of a long day. On the other was the opposition, a group of military men wearing an array of gleaming medals on starched khaki uniforms. It wasn't surprising that the SLORC began writing and reporting that the flowers in The Lady's hair were proof of her "narcissism and her need for the adoration of the crowds."

That she wore flowers in her hair was just the first criticism of Suu Kyi the SLORC dreamed up. They made constant references to the fact that Daw Suu Kyi had not lived in Burma for most of her adult life and, therefore, was unable to understand all the problems indigenous to the country. "After her father passed away," General Khin Nyunt maintained, "Aung San Suu Kyi accompanied her mother who was appointed Ambassador to India. Later Suu Kyi left for London. From the age of fourteen, she has drifted away from our country. She eventually married an Englishman and became even more apart from the country."

In response, U Bo Hla Tint, the Finance Minister of the exiled National League for Democracy party in Washington, D.C., argues, "If you look back, Suu Kyi was a child when she went to India with her mother, who was appointed Ambassador by the Burmese government. When Suu Kyi went to New York and worked at the United Nations, U Thant, who of course was also Burmese, was Secretary General. As far as marrying a foreigner, there are no restrictions in the Buddhist religion. You can marry anyone you like. We respect each other."

The most vicious rumor that the SLORC spread around the country, however, concerned the prize money that Aung San Suu Kyi collected. According to the state-run newspaper and the state-run television, the money went directly to Daw Suu Kyi's husband in England, who promptly bought a new house.

The truth is quite another story. Every cent that Daw Suu Kyi gained from the Nobel Peace Prize—as well as from the Sakharov Prize, which she also won—went into the Burma Trust for Health and Education. Created by Daw Suu Kyi and Michael Aris, and managed by a firm of accountants and a board of trustees in England, the income from the trust is designated for various educational and health projects in Burma, as well as for humanitarian aid to ethnic minorities and refugees.

* * *

At the time that Daw Suu Kyi won the Nobel Prize, an entire pro-democracy movement had already been built around her image and name. Further, from 1988 until 1991, an epidemic of democracy was spreading throughout the world—even South Africa was on its way to freedom, equality, and a democratic government. Feeling increasingly threatened, and in response to an overwhelming surge of publicity and attention, the SLORC began devising new ways not only to diminish Daw Suu Kyi's physical presence, but also to negate what it called "The Lady's self-imposed martyr state."

The SLORC not only closed University Avenue more frequently, prohibiting people from visiting Daw Suu Kyi, but they also prevented her—on many occasions—from leaving her compound, and cancelled her weekly gateside meetings. Once again, the SLORC miscalculated the reaction of the Burmese people, in much the same way that they had misjudged the people when they announced that Daw Suu Kyi was ineligible to run for public office. Before long, the military realized that any criticism or confinement of Daw Suu Kyi not only strengthened the resolve of the pro-democracy movement, but also brought increasing condemnation of Burma by the rest of the world.

If Aung San Suu Kyi became a prisoner of the Nobel Prize, the SLORC became the captive of their own prisoner.

Sometime during those six years, Aung San Suu Kyi entered menopause. It was an occurrence, she claimed, that did nothing more than make her acutely aware that time was limited for her to accomplish what she had set out to do. "I only kept thinking that I wished I had been put in detention at a younger age, so that after my release I would have a longer period to work." But while Daw Suu Kyi felt that time was finite when it came to achieving democracy in Burma, she also came to believe that time was infinite when it came to her detention. With tireless effort, her supporters tried to force the SLORC to admit that she had been incarcerated only because of her growing popularity and the threat that she posed to the regime.

In a complete change of attitude, more than two years after Daw Suu Kyi had been awarded the Nobel Peace Prize, General Than Shwe, the SLORC's chief, and General Khin Nyunt, its first secretary, invited Aung San Suu Kyi to a government guest house for a meeting. It would be the first time she would leave her compound since she had been confined. Broadcast over the state-controlled television were images of Daw Suu Kyi, dressed in a pink *longyi*, standing between a beaming General Than Shwe and an obviously delighted General Khin Nyunt. Although a camera recorded the surroundings—a teak-paneled room with plush chairs and sofas facing each other in two neat rows—and the smiles and warm greetings between Daw Suu Kyi and her hosts, the words of the trio were obscured by a voice-over that described for the public what was happening. If ever lip-readers were needed, it was certainly on that auspicious occasion. Later, Daw Suu Kyi would describe the two men in the following way: "General Than Shwe seemed very direct and honest, while General Khin Nyunt was very charming, in an Asian way."

After the Burmese people had recovered from their surprise and amazement, they were suddenly optimistic that perhaps the government was finally prepared to recognize The Lady and negotiate some kind of settlement with the National League for Democracy party. For the international community, including those who had business interests in Rangoon as well as foreign governments who had tried to pressure the SLORC into a dialogue with Daw Suu Kyi, it was the first positive sign that the two opposing sides were perhaps on the verge of coming to some sort of reconciliation. It was not to be.

During my meeting with General Khin Nyunt in Rangoon, he explained the reasons for that meeting. "We considered the meeting a family reunion. A spirit of *metta* [Buddhist spirit of goodwill] was with us in the room that day."

When asked why that meeting wasn't followed by The Lady's immediate release, he replied, "Because we were well aware of the dangers to this country caused by a communist conspiracy. Unfortunately, Aung San Suu Kyi had been thrust into the leadership role unknowingly by people who did not want democracy for Myanmar, but only power for themselves."

And when asked what the point was of meeting with Aung San Suu Kyi during her confinement, and broadcasting it on television, General Khin Nyunt continued, "As I have mentioned to you, we love and respect General Aung San and since Suu Kyi is his daughter, we also have a special attachment to her as the daughter of our national hero."

The "attachment" that General Khin Nyunt claimed that the SLORC had toward The Lady was made even more evident when there was no indication of when she would be released.

Ken Weideman, the Chargés d'Affaires at the United States Embassy in Rangoon, arrived at his post in 1996, after Daw Suu Kyi had already been released. He analyzed the situation in the following way. "All along, during any negotiation or meeting, the military government had the advantage of 'walk-away' power. And something else is very crucial, and that was that the SLORC was not about to admit all of a sudden that they were the bad guys, liberate Suu Kyi, and retreat back to the barracks."

At the beginning of 1994, after Aung San Suu Kyi had been under house arrest for more than four and a half years, cracks began to appear in the SLORC's position. The country's economy was finally beginning to show some encouraging signs of life under the stimulus of free-market forces. As foreign investment began to enter Burma, the SLORC realized that any concurrent technological improvement was simply not going to happen unless the military regime received massive infusions of aid from Japan, as well as funding from multilateral institutions such as the World Bank and the International Monetary Fund. To their dismay, they began to accept the fact that Aung San Suu Kyi was the linchpin. As long as the SLORC kept The Lady under house arrest, not only was foreign aid unlikely to be forthcoming, but even more serious consequences would follow, such as harsh condemnation by the United Nations Commission on Human-Rights. In fact, several members of the United States House of Representatives were ready to submit a bill calling for a full-scale trade and investment embargo, similar to the embargo that had been used in South Africa. In the hope of avoiding a wave of international censure, but not prepared to go the distance and release Daw Suu Kyi, the SLORC deviated from its policy and allowed her to receive a visitor other than a family member.

Congressman Bill Richardson, a Democrat from New Mexico and the current American Ambassador to the United Nations, was known and respected for his one-man peacekeeping missions throughout the world under the Clinton administration. Richardson's repeated requests to meet with General Khin Nyunt and with Aung San Suu Kyi were finally granted. Daw Suu Kyi, still wary of accepting favors from the regime, however, imposed certain conditions when the government approached her with what they claimed was their intiative. "I agreed to meet with Mr. Richardson," Daw Suu Kyi explains, "but only in the company of a United Nations official and a reporter from *The New York Times*."

Jehan Raheem, the representative in Burma from the United Nations Development Program, was permitted to attend the meeting as the representative from the United Nations, but instead of a *New York Times* reporter, an official from the United States Embassy in Rangoon was sent in to take notes.

For three hours, Suu Kyi conferred with her visitors. One of the first things that she made clear to then-Congressman Richardson was that releasing her would not be enough unless the SLORC completely changed its position and recognized the results of the 1991 elections. Daw Suu Kyi's terms were specific: the SLORC must relinquish power and turn the government over to those who had been elected and were the people's choice.

In response to Richardson's question about the SLORC's apparent willingness to engage in a dialogue with her and others from her political party, Daw Suu Kyi said, "They [the SLORC] have made no moves to have a dialogue of any kind except on the terms under which I would leave Burma. And that is not a dialogue. That is a monologue."

After conferring with Daw Suu Kyi, Richardson played shuttle diplomacy and went to see General Khin Nyunt, ostensibly to persuade the SLORC to open a realistic dialogue. "I believe a process of possible talks has been started," Richardson announced at the time. "The key to Burma's ability to improve its international reputation with the United States and the outside world is Aung San Suu Kyi."

Upon his return to Daw Suu Kyi's house the following day, Richardson was forced to admit that so far he had not made any progress in getting the SLORC to agree to a dialogue. Richardson did, however, present Daw Suu Kyi with a letter from President Clinton, advising her that when Congressman Richardson returned in several days after meeting again with General Khin Nyunt, he (President Clinton) expected a response from the SLORC that would set down new conditions to begin a dialogue.

Once again, Richardson went to see General Khin Nyunt. But when he came back to consult with Daw Suu Kyi for what would be the final time, he was forced to report that the SLORC had categorically refused to make any concessions.

"It must be very exhausting for the SLORC to go on lying," Daw Suu Kyi said to Richardson. "Elections were promised, elections were held, and yet the military holds onto power despite its defeat at the polls. The people feel cheated."

Eventually, the conversation turned to the National Convention. It was then that Congressman Richardson asked Daw Suu Kyi if it was possible that the regime was making efforts toward democracy.

"It's an absolute farce," Daw Suu Kyi answered adamantly, "The National Convention makes no sense at all because the people are not allowed to speak, and if they are just there to nod their heads, there's nothing. It's not a convention. I cannot accept it as something that seriously represents the will of the people at all."

When her visitors were preparing to leave, Aung San Suu Kyi accompanied them, leading them through the entrance hall where banners on which the words of her father, General Aung San, were written. Pointing to one, Richardson asked what it meant. Daw Suu Kyi translated the words from Burmese to English.

"You cannot use martial law as an excuse for injustice," she read the words quietly.

Pondering the meaning for a moment, Congressman Richardson wondered, "Are the signs put there for the benefit of any military visitors?"

Daw Suu Kyi shrugged. "Perhaps the words might somehow educate some of my visitors," she replied.

As the Congressman shook her hand, he asked, "How would you define yourself?"

Daw Suu Kyi did not hesitate. "I think the authorities know that I will be active politically because I look upon myself as a politician." She smiled. "And that isn't a dirty word, is it, Congressman?"

14

IN WHAT COULD be best described as an extended mood of benevolence, after Congressman Richardson's visit with Aung San Suu Kyi, the SLORC allowed another nonfamily member into the compound on University Avenue. Rewata Dhamma was the venerable Buddhist monk who had first met Daw Suu Kyi and her mother in India when Daw Khin Kyi was the Burmese Ambassador there, and later met Suu Kyi again in Oxford with her husband, two sons, and several Tibetan Lamas at a Buddhist Temple.

Between May 1994 and January 1995, the SLORC allowed the monk to visit Daw Suu Kyi on three occasions, and for a while, it looked as if he was on the verge of brokering an accord with the SLORC for her release.

"On my first visit to Suu Kyi, sometime in the summer of 1994," Rewata Dhamma recalls, "she told me that she wanted national reconciliation. Her exact words were, 'democracy is not something you get from others. You have to build it yourself. If Nelson Mandela could work with whites, I can work with the SLORC.' That was the message that I communicated to the regime in the hope that they would consider that their previous calls for reconciliation and dialogue were finally being answered in a positive way."

In January 1995, however, on what would be Rewata Dhamma's last visit with the Nobel Prize laureate while she was still under house arrest, he reported quite a different story to the international press. According to the monk, when he broached the subject of a possible dialogue with the SLORC, Daw Suu Kyi announced that she had changed her mind. "You came too late," she allegedly told the Buddhist monk, "I'm no longer interested in having any dialogue with them at all."

Daw Suu Kyi's response, as reported by the monk, baffled not only her colleagues, but also the international community in Rangoon who had become increasingly optimistic that the stalemate between the two political entities was ending. There were too many people working behind the scenes, helping Rewata Dhamma come to an agreement with the SLORC to liberate The Lady, while at the same time ensuring that the regime did not appear to have succumbed either to international pressure or political weakness. These were the same people who, for months, had been instrumental in securing permission from the regime for the monk to shuttle back and forth between General Khin Nyunt and Aung San Suu Kyi in order to work out terms for a compromise. There was little doubt at the time that negotiations were going along smoothly, and The Lady's release was imminent.

When Daw Suu Kyi purportedly refused to begin a dialogue with the SLORC, something didn't make sense.

Aung San Suu Kyi had always maintained before and during her house arrest that she welcomed a dialogue with the SLORC. "It is far better to argue with words," Daw Suu Kyi has always said, "than to shoot each other with guns."

One foreign diplomat posted in Rangoon at the time told me, "Any experienced leader understands that negotiation is the key to understanding, which in turn results in political compromise. It was hard to believe that Aung San Suu Kyi would have refused a dialogue, especially when she could have used the Nobel Prize to force the SLORC into discussions."

During the time I spent in Rangoon, I had occasion to interview several of those people who had worked behind the scenes to arrange what should have become a dialogue between the

SLORC and The Lady. According to them, Rawata Dhamma had indeed come to Rangoon in good faith—to liberate Daw Suu Kyi and to secure the SLORC's agreement that a dialogue would begin. After numerous meetings with the SLORC, however, and the realization that the monk's dream to build a pagoda in Rangoon would become a reality only if he somehow misinterpreted Aung San Suu Kyi's desire to begin that dialogue, the result was a deadlock. Predictably, the SLORC used that bit of propaganda to place the blame squarely on Daw Suu Kyi.

While pro-democracy advocates inside Burma were disheartened by Daw Suu Kyi's apparent hard-line position toward the SLORC, pro-democracy and human-rights groups outside the country applauded her intransigence. One member of the NLD in Burma claimed that The Lady was less preoccupied by a very real need to come to an agreement with the SLORC so that hundreds of political prisoners could be liberated from prison, than she was impressed and influenced by the power and money behind the Burma Project in New York. "The NLD government-in-exile in Washington, as well as the multi-million-dollar Burma Project group sponsored by George Soros," the NLD member explained, "sent strong messages that any compromise by Daw Suu Kyi would be tantamount to legitimatizing an illegitimate regime. Once Suu won the Nobel Peace Prize, pro-democracy groups in exile believed that it was only a question of time before the SLORC would have to give in. In the minds of the people in New York and Washington, there was no need for negotiation with the military regime, since they had already won the battle."

While the pro-democracy groups in exile were correct in believing that they had indeed won the battle for international support, what they failed to understand was that without a dialogue with the SLORC, the Burmese people would continue to live in misery or languish in prison. Still, those same exiled pro-democracy and human-rights groups, often intellectually elitist, unrealistic, and certainly out of touch with the day-to-day conditions in Burma, nonetheless managed to create the most successful and high-tech political movement in history.

Unlike the Palestinian Revolution in the 1980s, which used terrorism as the most cost-effective weapon against civilians to make their cause known, the Burmese pro-democracy groups in exile devised a method for reaching and informing millions of people throughout the world on the current political situation in Burma under the SLORC without firing a shot, hijacking an airplane, launching a grenade, or even leaving their offices.

Learning of a Burma web site on the Internet, millions of people who had never even heard of Burma suddenly became aware of a certain Nobel Peace Prize winner who was relentless in her vocal opposition against a military regime with a 400,000-man army, equipped with the most modern and sophisticated weapons, that had taken over the country by force.

Still, regardless of how much global recognition, and financial support, the pro-democracy movement garnered that kept the cause alive, only those who lived inside the country were in a position to understand the inherent strengths and weakness of the regime.

The stalemate continued between the NLD and the SLORC until, on July 11, 1995, without warning, Aung San Suu Kyi's house arrest ended as abruptly as it had begun.

In an extraordinary and unheralded policy reversal, Colonel Kyaw Win, the SLORC's deputy chief of military intelligence, drove to the house on University Avenue to inform Aung San Suu Kyi that the SLORC was reinstating her freedom without preconditions. Before Daw Suu Kyi was prepared to accept the SLORC's decision, however, she made it very clear to Colonel Kyaw Win that she remained committed to the cause of democracy, and would not consider any secret deals having to do with her release. Daw Suu Kyi describes her first thought after Colonel Kyaw Win left that day. "My father always said to hope for the best, but be prepared for the worst," she says quietly. "Suddenly my father's words meant something important to me. In my case, after I was released, I realized that nothing had changed except that I was free to walk outside."

Within hours of Daw Suu Kyi's release, a small crowd, surprisingly calm and restrained, gathered in front of the house on University Avenue, waiting for The Lady to make an appearance. Finally, she appeared and made a brief statement.

"I have always believed that the future stability and happiness of our nation depends entirely on the readiness of all parties to work for reconciliation. During the years that I spent under house arrest, many parts of the world have undergone almost unbelievable change, and all changes for the better were brought about through dialogue. [It] has been the key to a happy resolution of long-festering problems. Once bitter enemies in South Africa are now working together for the betterment of their people. Why can't we look forward to a similar process? We have to choose between dialogue or utter devastation. There is more in common between the authorities and we of the democratic forces in Burma than existed between the black and white peoples of South Africa. Extreme viewpoints are not confined to any particular group and it is the responsibility of the leaders to control such elements that threaten the spirit of reconciliation."

The next day a larger crowd gathered and still a larger one the day after, waiting in silent vigil until finally several of her supporters hoisted Daw Suu Kyi up onto a desk on top of the gate surrounding her compound. It was the beginning of what would become a unique political institution—Aung San Suu Kyi's gate-side meetings in Rangoon.

On the third day of freedom, Daw Suu Kyi once again made a speech in which she called for a dialogue with the SLORC that would lead to some kind of reconciliation. "I'm not that different a person now after six years," Daw Suu Kyi told the jubilant crowd, "although I believe that I am spiritually stronger. If I've mellowed, I'm pleased, since people should mellow with age, and I hope I will be aging gracefully. I would like to think that detention changed me or it would have been a waste of six years." And then, making a subtle illusion to her opponents, she added, "There are those who pride themselves on never changing but I am not sure that's anything to be proud of. People say there's something new in the fact that I'm calling for a dialogue with the SLORC, but that isn't true. I've always asked for a dialogue. Only discipline and courage devoid of any grudge will help us achieve our desired aims and aspirations. Pro-democracy forces should work slowly, steadily, thoughtfully, and courageously."

If Daw Suu Kyi expected that the SLORC would welcome a dialogue with unabashed restraint, she was wrong. In fact, not only did the SLORC ignore her political advances, but the regime also ignored her release. There was no official statement issued by the regime, not even in the government-controlled newspaper, *The New Light of Myanmar*. When questioned about her release, the editor-in-chief of the newspaper simply replied, "We've heard rumors but we have no facts."

Judging by the veil of secrecy that seemed to surround the event, it appeared as if the SLORC was not even interested in garnering world praise for releasing Burma's most famous pro-democracy dissident. Eventually, the news of Daw Suu Kyi's release was broadcast in the foreign press even before her family was officially notified.

When Michael Aris was approached by the British media, his response was circumspect and cautious as he issued a statement from his house in Oxford. "I am waiting to get confirmation of her release from various sources. Whether or not I receive confirmation, I know that it is my wife's wish that I do not give any comment in public." In response to reporters' questions about whether Aung San Suu Kyi would be returning to her family in England, Michael said, "Although I last saw her in January, and haven't spoken to her since, I am sure that if she is released she would not be coming home to Britain. She has far too much work to do over there."

Several hours later when Michael was again questioned as to the validity of the rumor that his wife was free, he said, "I am hopeful that rumors of my wife's release are true. But at the moment, we are still waiting to hear it from her own lips."

It would be several days before Michael would hear from Suu Kyi directly, and when he did, their conversation would fuel more rumors concerning the state of their marriage.

Daw Suu Kyi's routine after she was released indicated that she was telling the truth when she stated that other than being allowed to venture outside her compound, nothing else had changed. In the days that followed, Daw Suu Kyi made one quick trip to the optician to get her eyes checked. Other than that one foray out of the compound, she spent her time going from one meeting to the next, conferring with supporters and colleagues who had flocked to the house to discuss the NLD's future strategy. At one point she remarked to an aide that she had not yet spoken to her husband or sons. The fact was that the telephone lines in Daw Suu Kyi's house had not yet been reinstated by the government. "I should really get away somewhere quiet with a telephone," she sighed, before disappearing behind another closed-door conference. Finally, arrangements were made for Daw Suu Kyi to go to the home of a British diplomat where she would receive a telephone call from her husband and her younger son. According to Daw Suu Kyi, when the conversation with Michael and Kim finally happened, it was surprisingly matter-of-fact. "He said hello and I said hello and then we talked about his plans," Daw Suu Kyi recalls.

A British journalist who happened to be at the diplomat's house when Daw Suu Kyi spoke to her husband and son, openly criticized her for what he termed was her "frighteningly dispassionate, even faintly robotic attitude toward her family."

"The impression I got," the journalist says, "is that when she talked about her family, it was as if she was reading from a manual on western emotions. And, when she finally talked to her family, it seemed more out of a sense of duty than a desire."

The British diplomat, however, at whose house Daw Suu Kyi received her husband's call that day vehemently disagrees. "I suspect that the pain of separation was no less acute for Suu Kyi than for anyone else. The only difference is that she had six long years to grow accustomed to that separation. What happened to her was that she learned to steel herself against the pain somewhere very deep inside of her. Her attitude was no less than an exercise in discipline much like her ability to go on a hunger strike or to meditate each and every day while in captivity."

Yet, despite any self-taught ability to mask her pain, Daw Suu Kyi was quite pragmatic when she expressed her feelings concerning her family and any hope she might have harbored of returning to her role as a wife and mother. "I don't think I will have a normal family life for a very long time," she admitted sadly. "In the beginning, when I realized that our lives would never be the same it depressed me. But eventually I managed to overcome the depression and stop feeling lonely or sorry for myself. Any pain I felt at the separation, or any longing I had to see Michael and the children simply became part of my daily life."

Since Aung San Suu Kyi's release, not only has the state of her marriage been a topic of SLORC conversation, but the emotional state of her children as well. According to several government sources, Alexander, the older son, suffered an emotional breakdown while at George Washington University in Washington, D.C., and has since transferred to a smaller and less high-profile college in the Midwest of the United States.

As for Kim, the younger son, SLORC propaganda continues to portray him as a "decadent youth, influenced by the drug and music culture of the West."

In defense of the Aris boys, family members and close friends claim that while Alexander did, in fact, transfer to another university, he is in "fine and stable shape and doing very well academically," while Kim is busy "pursuing his interest in the arts and music and happily enjoying the usual activities of any normal young man, including the company of a new girlfriend."

As for the political rumors surrounding Daw Suu Kyi's release, General Ne Win was once again the focus of discussion.

From the beginning, the abruptness of the SLORC's decision provoked the speculation that it had been General Ne Win who had orchestrated the change in the SLORC's policy to release Aung San Suu Kyi. One pro-democracy advocate says simply, "Anytime something happens that is totally out of character with the regime, or completely out of the blue, you can always assume that it comes from Ne Win."

*   *   *

According to several well-placed intelligence sources within the military, about a year before Suu Kyi was released from house arrest, General Ne Win went by helicopter to the Pyay area in the north of Burma to visit his hometown of Prome. A highly superstitious and religious man, Ne Win instructed the helicopter pilot to circle the pagoda nine times before landing. After the craft touched down, Ne Win went to the town hall where he was received as a highly honored guest and where he was asked to sign a book reserved for special dignitaries. Ne Win wrote in the book, "Dear God, in all my future lives, please make sure that I never have to deal with or have anything to do with such people as I am now involved with who are leading my country."

Based on Ne Win's well-known fears that the SLORC was getting too powerful, too economically sound, and too forgetful about who had put them where they were, the story fuels the rumors that it was General Ne Win who decided to release Aung San Suu Kyi after six years of house arrest.

As for that register in the town hall in Prome, it has since disappeared.

*   *   *

According to one Burmese who is close to certain members of the SLORC, to understand the ex-dictator's idiosyncratic and disturbed mind, it is essential to realize that Ne Win's only goal at the time was to unleash the most lethal obstacle in the path of the regime. "The decision to release The Lady was last-minute. Only several days before it happened, the SLORC had a meeting where they unanimously decided to renew her arrest for another six months. It was General Ne Win who pressured the SLORC into releasing her because he believed that once free, she would revert to her old ways. There is no doubt that Ne Win still has sufficient power and there is also no doubt that he continues to hate the SLORC."

Intelligence sources within the SLORC, however, categorically deny that General Ne Win had anything to do with the decision to release her. Instead, they claim that The Lady's release had been under consideration by Senior General Than Shwe and General Khin Nyunt for well over a year. One SLORC member told me that the government believed that "sufficient progress had been made at the National Convention for the good of the country, so that releasing The Lady would not have an adverse effect on the efforts being made to draft a new constitution."

David Young at the U.S. Department of State agrees with that reasoning on the part of the SLORC. "Basically, the SLORC felt sufficiently unthreatened that Daw Suu Kyi would ever become a bonafide leader," Young explains, "especially since they added that clause into the new constitution that precluded her from ever taking public office based on the fact that she is married to a foreigner and lived out of Burma for more than twenty years."

As for Aung San Suu Kyi, she claims not to understand who ordered that her house arrest be terminated or why. "I doubt that even the authorities themselves can say why," Daw Suu Kyi says. "In the end, you don't know how far you are influenced by your surroundings here in Rangoon and all the rumors that go around, and what you actually hear or what you are told. It's just difficult to separate rumors from the truth."

More cynical viewpoints of Daw Suu Kyi's release were that the SLORC needed to demonstrate their good intentions to the West, namely to the World Bank and the International Monetary Fund, which had cut off aid to the regime in 1988, based on its abominable human-rights record in quelling the riots and demonstrations.

Notwithstanding the involvement of General Ne Win, the most widely accepted reason for Aung San Suu Kyi's release is that the SLORC understood that the economic future of Burma depended not only on infusions of direct foreign investment, but also on a "resumption of aid from multilateral agencies."

Scott Rosenberg of the Brooker Group, a business and trade consultancy that specializes in the Mekong River countries of Thailand, Burma, Laos, Vietnam, and Cambodia, agrees. "Only then can Burma aspire to compete with its Southeast Asian neighbors. In fact, after helping to engineer Aung San Suu Kyi's release, Japan became the first government to hold out the prospect of renewed financial aid to Burma."

Yogei Kono, the Japanese Foreign Minister at the time of Daw Suu Kyi's release, announced that Japan would be willing to start talks with the Burmese government on the resumption of official yen loans that had been suspended during the military coup in 1988. When the announcement came of Daw Suu Kyi's release, the Japanese government made it known that they considered the SLORC's actions to be a sign that they intended to pursue moderate policies. Although Tokyo was somewhat instrumental in securing Daw Suu Kyi's release by promising renewed aid, the truth is that even before she was released—in March of that year—one billion yen were sent to Burma for emergency agricultural aid.

Since July 1995, Aung San Suu Kyi has remained committed to the cause of democracy despite the continued suppression of free speech and the ongoing repression of many pro-democracy leaders by the SLORC. Speaking out when the SLORC allows her, she still tries to appear on Saturday afternoons, answering questions, smiling, and above all, warning the people of Burma that the future will not be "all that smooth." "You have to suffer to get your goals," she repeats again and again.

Concerning her own goals, Daw Suu Kyi is always careful to qualify her aspirations when she tells the people or the press, "As long as I can be of use to the people, I will continue. One thing I vowed while I was under house arrest was that I was never never going to let summary arrests and human-rights abuse go on happening. There is no doubt in my mind that the pro-democracy forces in Burma are now stronger and better prepared to stop that kind of thing. If the Burmese people love someone like my father or myself, they really will take that person to their hearts and they will forgive a lot as long as they are convinced that we are sincere and we have their good in mind. But there is a limit to their forgiveness and that's a good thing. At any rate, I feel spiritually stronger and I think that I have learned to put a much greater value on compassion, which is very important in today's world."

15

A POLOGISTS FOR THE SLORC, western business people who consider Burma to be a candy store of investment opportunity, argue that the concept of human-rights as we know them in the Occident is not applicable in all cultures.

Those westerners who judge the SLORC positively do so on the basis of the regime's willingness to overlook many irregular business practices. It is not surprising that those same investors consider Burma to be the ideal place to invest, since the SLORC disregards reciprocal international tax treaties, forgives unacceptable safety standards of heavy machinery, and generally ignores abhorrent conditions in the workplace. The cost of doing business in Burma for the foreign investor is, therefore, kept to a minimum. Those companies and private investors who have already entrenched themselves throughout the country in various industrial and corporate enterprises have made, and will continue to make, exorbitant profits. So does the SLORC. In addition to paying for permits and other official permission to work inside the country, foreign corporations also share a percentage of all revenues with the regime.

Michael Dobbs-Higginson, a South African who still describes himself as a Rhodesian, and who represents Japanese business interests in Burma, says, "Looking at Asian regional history since World War II, it is interesting to note many of today's economic successes in Asia. . . . Most have been largely the result of strong authoritarian governments, often military in origin, which impose order and discipline to create the structural building blocks for economic and social development. When analyzing individual Asian countries, most of us forget that each evolves at a different speed in the direction of economic development. Only then is democracy possible."

The SLORC will readily admit—and with pride—that it has put financial growth and international investment first on its agenda. "Bringing Burma on a par with developed countries is our primary goal," Colonel Hla Min says. "That is what we believe will make our people happy."

Human-rights and democracy, according to the SLORC, are by-products of a healthy economy.

Traveling through Burma today leaves no doubt that there has never been as much foreign investment pouring into the country as during the last five years—and not just in major cities such as Rangoon, Mandalay, and Taunggyi. Throughout rural areas as well, international gas pipelines, bridges, and railroads are all under construction. Ironically, those countries with the biggest financial investment in Burma are often the countries most critical of the regime.

For instance, France is the second largest investor with foreign capital of approximately $465 million, while the United Kingdom has an investment of more than $798 million, and the United States, the most vocal critic of human-rights abuses in Burma, has an investment of $243 million. Other countries that criticize the SLORC in the front rooms but make financial deals in the back rooms are Australia with an investment of $30 million; Austria, $70 million; Canada, $25 million; Denmark, $14 million; and The Netherlands with an investment of $83 million.

Those countries that invest in Burma but are less hypocritical in their official position toward the SLORC are China, Burma's largest new arms supplier, with an investment of $6 million; Singapore, with $607 million; Japan, $128 million; and Thailand, with $422 million.

The most spectacular project under construction in Burma is the Yadana natural gas pipeline project, which has become the focal point of domestic and international debate. Financed by companies in the United States, France, and Thailand, the pipeline has raised serious concerns about human-rights abuses and forced labor connected to its construction, as well as international environmental concerns and the rights of indigenous peoples to "control and exploit the resources in their traditional lands."

The Yadana field is a natural gas resource located fifty-five meters beneath the Andaman Sea, and about forty-three miles off the coast of Burma. Approximately 220 miles of the pipeline will be underwater, and the last 30 miles will traverse the Tenasserim region, which is inhabited by ethnic and indigenous groups in Burma.

UNOCAL, an American petroleum company in partnership with TOTAL, a French company, has entered into a joint venture with the SLORC to construct a gas pipeline from the Yadana field in Burma's Gulf of Martaban that will extend to the Thai border. Thailand, the principal buyer of gas, has signed a thirty-year contract through its state petroleum company, the Petroleum Authority of Thailand (PTT), agreeing to purchase Yadana gas from the Burmese state petroleum company, the Myanma Oil and Gas Enterprise (MOGE). Once the pipeline begins production, which will be sometime during 1998, the SLORC will receive an estimated $400 million a year in revenue.

According to a 1996 Country Report on Human-Rights Practices in Burma compiled by the United States Department of State, Burma, although a poor country with an average per capita gross domestic product of about $200 to $300 a year, has substantial mineral, fishing, and timber resources. After twenty-six years of isolation, in 1988 the SLORC has begun slowly to open up the country in an effort to attract foreign investment. As a result there has been some economic improvement, although the same administrative obstacles continue to exist: restrictions on private commerce, the constant changing of rules and regulations, overcentralized decision making, a bloated bureaucracy, a greatly overvalued currency, poor infrastructure, and grossly disproportionate military spending.

Until now, despite considerable foreign investment and massive industrial development, the only section of society to benefit from foreign investment has been the SLORC business traders, and international investors. The SLORC assures the Burmese people that not only will they eventually benefit from all the progress being made throughout the country, but as soon as Burma emerges from developing-nation status, they will also enjoy a democratic system of government with full human-rights and liberties.

From a purely cynical point of view, the most obvious question is why would the SLORC step down and call for elections just when the fruits of their labors, especially the UNOCAL/ TOTAL pipeline, start bringing in millions of dollars of annual income?

Aung San Suu Kyi maintains that the quality of life for the average Burmese has not changed at all, not even in proportion to the progress that has already been made throughout the country. "I would like to know how the presence of TOTAL and all the other multinational investment affects the country," Aung San Suu Kyi asks. "And by that, I mean the people who need it most? Foreign investment, foreign companies, what are they doing for the common people? Have they really benefited the common people in any way, this is something which has yet to be proved. Does this just mean more money and more wealth for those who already have wealth and money? Does it mean more privileges for the elite, or does it mean real change in the situation of the common people? I think we need more proof on this before we decide."

Also contained in the report written by the United States Department of State is the following statement: "... despite the appearance of greater normalcy fostered by increased economic activity, the SLORC's severe repression of human-rights continues unchanged.... Out of sight of most visitors, citizens continue to live subject at any time and without appeal to the arbitrary and sometimes brutal dictates of the military. There continue to be credible reports, particularly from ethnic minority–dominated areas, that soldiers committed serious human-rights abuses, including extrajudicial killings and rape. Disappearances continue, and members of the security forces beat and otherwise abuse detainees."

According to reliable sources, 30,000 ethnic Burmese, Mons, Karens, and Tavoyans from more than fifty villages in the districts of Ye Byu, Thayet Chaung, and Tavoy have been forcibly displaced from their homes since the beginning of 1991. Those same sources also claim the inhabitants of Migyaunglaung, a town situated in the immediate vicinity of the pipeline, were deported or fled over the Thai border in 1992, to make room for a communication committee that had been set up by TOTAL.

The Electricity Generating Authority of Thailand, which operates the power plant in charge of converting the Yadana gas into electricity, has publicly acknowledged that construction of the pipeline required forced relocation of villages. Yet, in an interview with several executives from TOTAL in France, they categorically denied that any relocation of the population took place, claiming that the "area is sparsely populated . . . no relocation should be necessary on the route of the pipeline."

TOTAL does admit, however, that prior to their contract with the SLORC, forced relocations did take place "probably" through the Three Pagoda Pass, which is north of the Tavoy and Zin Ba river valleys. "We had a choice of several possible routes," a TOTAL executive explains, "and we agreed unanimously on that one. But we have no say in any land matters since according to Burmese law, all land belongs to the state. TOTAL does not have the authority to proceed with the expropriation of land nor with guaranteeing that land remains with any group in that area."

While TOTAL relieves themselves of all responsibility of forced locations before July 1992 when they signed the contract with the SLORC, reliable sources in the area dispute that claim. According to an ethnic leader in the immediate vicinity of the pipeline, villages within fifty kilometers of the pipeline have been razed by the SLORC, more as a precaution against terrorist activities than to liberate land for the project. Apparently, the military regime perceived these areas to be possible shelters for ethnic Karen and Mon opposition groups that could try to destroy the pipeline.

As for forced labor used on the Yadana project, according to *The New Light of Myanmar* newspaper, there are approximately 4 million "voluntary" workers who contribute their efforts in building a better infrastructure.

Other sources at the newspaper, however, claim that forced labor is used by the military junta to prepare the country for the tourist season, particularly building hotels, repairing monuments, and sprucing up various shrines and pagodas.

Even more dangerous in the rural areas, especially where the Yadana pipeline is currently under construction, is that often military and economic interests converge. For example, as the pipeline helps the army maintain and spread its control over certain rural regions, construction of roads and railways allows the army to penetrate even farther into those areas held by rebel forces. By explaining to the villagers around Kanbauk, for example, that it was neccessary to protect the pipeline by building military barracks, the army forced civilians to work without pay "for their own good, as well as for the good of the country."

The TOTAL executive in charge of coordinating the construction in Burma and Thailand is Hervé Chagnoux. He summed it up best when he said, "I cannot guarantee that the military is not using forced labor. All we can really guarantee are the contracts we make ourselves, the people we employ on our own.... But if there is forced labor on the construction site, it is not out of spite or malice that the SLORC are obliged to use it."

Aung San Suu Kyi has consistently maintained that, "We, in the National League for Democracy, believe that human-rights are of universal relevance. But even those who do not believe in human-rights must certainly agree that the rule of law is most important. Without the rule of law there can be no peace, not in a nation, a region, or throughout the world. In Burma at the moment there is no rule of law, which means there can be no peace or justice in this country."

As already mentioned, another goal of the SLORC is to sustain the state physically without any threat of disunity or rebellion from the more than 135 ethnic groups and nationalities that are dispersed along the border and in rural areas.

If the regime consistently relocates ethnic minorities to make room for projects such as the Yadana pipeline, or railroads, or bridges, it is fair to assume that not only are the ethnic minorities *not* benefitting from any economic progress, but they are actually suffering as a result of it.

If the SLORC forces ethnic minorities who live in the rural areas to work as porters for the army, or work to build various government projects without pay, economic progress is clearly at the detriment and expense of the Burmese people.

In January 1997, during my second trip to Burma, and in the company of two members of a Swedish human-rights group, I traveled to the Thai side of the Burmese/Thailand border to visit several refugee camps. Most of the people living there had only recently fled from Burma, and were either Karen, Karenni, or Shan nationality. Each one of the eight people that I interviewed—three men, three women, and two children approximately sixteen years of age—made similar allegations that violence against ethnic minorities by the Burmese Army units stationed in their areas occurred.

According to them, "Civilians were killed or severely beaten by Burmese troops for disobeying orders, such as refusing to work because of illness, or in one case, because a woman was heavily pregnant ... tortured by soldiers because families refused to leave their homes and possessions, while others were lined up and executed by soldiers after accusations of collaboration with insurgent forces in the same area." Not only did these people talk into a tape recorder, but they also offered physical proof that left no doubt that they had been mutilated, beaten, burned, and disfigured.

During an interview with General David Abel, the affable Anglo-Burmese Minister for National Planning and Economic Development, I asked if there was any truth whatsoever to any of those charges. His reply. "Absolutely not. It is against the Buddhist religion, and we are very religious Buddhists in Myanmar. We would never harm or kill any living thing."

I asked if it was possible that the SLORC had perhaps made a mistake, for example, and some soldiers had acted violently, and since then, the general command had changed its policy in the border areas.

General Abel replied, "We are making very big efforts to develop the agricultural sector of the country, not only to increase exports but to provide enough food for all. In economic terms, all of those allegations are completely false and total nonsense."

When asked about the cast in human terms: How the SLORC explains all the marks these people have from being tortured, General Abel responded, "I cannot say that some of the different people who live in the border areas are not fighting amongst themselves, which they are. I cannot explain why they are acting in such inhuman ways toward one another."

And when asked why they would make these accusations against the SLORC, he said, "All I know is that the communists and insurgent groups are saying that it is the army that is doing this, and it is not the army. All the propaganda is coming from the NLD and The Lady in cahoots with these border criminals."

The fact that the SLORC claims to have their own version of a democratic system of government holds dangerous consequences for the Burmese people.

The United Nations *Special Rapporteur* was able to meet with or study the records of the following people who were sentenced to prison without trial by the SLORC.

U Ohn Kyaing, for instance, served seven years in Insein Prison for "sending a letter defying the authority of the SLORC." Often, he was forced to "sleep on cold cement," and never had enough to eat even though his family brought him food and medicine once a month. He says, "The guards usually took it."

Tin Aung Aung, Zaw Myint Aung, Saw Myint, and Hla Than each were sentenced without trial and all are currently serving twenty-five years in Insein Prison for "organizing a meeting for setting up an illegal parallel government."

In *Letters From Burma*, Aung San Suu Kyi poignantly describes the imprisonment of U Win Tin, the only member of the original Executive Committee of the NLD and one of the first pro-democracy leaders to be arrested by the SLORC.

A freelance writer and educator who believed in intellectual freedom and justice, U Win Tin was actively involved in the pro-democracy movement that spread throughout Burma in 1988. Initially charged with having a telephone conversation with the father of someone whom the SLORC declared was a "fugitive from the law," U Win Tin was interrogated, deprived of sleep, food, and medicine. According to Aung San Suu Kyi, ". . . his interrogators wished to force him to admit that he was my adviser on political tactics, in other words, that he was my puppet master."

U Win Tin, however, refused to make any false confession and, as a result, was sentenced to three years in prison in October 1989. In June 1992, when his term was due to end, the SLORC imposed an additional eleven-year sentence. In February 1994, Bill Richardson, then the Democratic Congressman from New Mexico, visited U Win Tin in prison and found him in bad physical condition, although his mind was clear and his spirits unwavering. Since November 1995 U Win Tin and twenty-seven other political prisoners have been charged with breaking prison rules, and will be forced to stand trial. Aung San Suu Kyi is afraid that U Win Tin might not survive a third prison sentence imposed on him by the SLORC.

During a meeting in my presence between the *Special Rapporteur* and several people who had served years in Insein Prison, the former prisoners maintained that they had been "tortured, beaten, shackled, and nearly suffocated . . . burned, stabbed, had salt and chemicals rubbed into open wounds, and endured psychological torture, including threats of death." According to several women who had been incarcerated, they had been raped, or used as porters, or in some cases, had suffered burns and the amputation of body parts. One woman couldn't tell me anything. She simply showed me that she had no tongue. A solider had cut it out.

Although the SLORC claims to be a united front, ruling in a democractic fashion where the majority vote is the decisive factor of any decision, recently there have been cracks in the regime, such as an assassination attempt on General Tin Oo, the SLORC Secretary Two.

Even before that particular act of violence within the ranks of the SLORC, divisions within the regime have always existed, although not always as blatantly obvious.

16

THE SIMPLE DEFINITION of the SLORC is that it is a military junta, comprised of twenty-two generals who virtually rule the country.

Senior General Thun Shwe holds the title of Chairman, while General Maung Aye is Vice Chairman. General Maung Aye is the army strongman, but it is the military intelligence chief, General Khin Nyuni, who is regarded as the key architect, known throughout the country simply as Secretary One. He is also the Chairman of the National Health Committee, the Union of Myanmar Privatisation Commission, and Central Committee of Myanmar Cultural Heritage Preservation, Restoration, and Conservation.

General Tin Oo is Secretary Two.

Other members of the SLORC, not necessarily by order of their importance, are General Maung Aye, Vice Chairman of the SLORC; Vice Admiral Maung Maung Khin; Lieutenant General Tin Tun; Lieutenant General Phone Myint; Lieutenant General Aung Ye Kyaw; Lieutenant General Sein Aung; Lieutenant General Chit Swe;Lieutenant General Kyaw Ba; Lieutenant General Maung Thint; Lieutenant General Myo Nyunt; Lieutenant General Myint Aung; Lieutenant General Mya Thin; Lieutenant General Thein Win; Lieutenant General Kyaw Min; Lieutenant General Aye Thaung; Lieutenant General Tun Kyi; Vice Admiral

Than Nyunt; Major General Soe Myint; and Major General Kyaw Than.

While pragmatism can best describe the SLORC's economic policies, and nepotism or favoritism has replaced any abstract notion of the political left and right, brutality has become a synonym for the regime. Nonetheless it is difficult to put the SLORC into a specific category, since there isn't any apparent *-ism* that describes their political philosophy—it is not communism, socialism, fascism, or capitalism. Yet, judging from a variety of reports and first-person testimony by internationally recognized human-rights groups, it would seem that the SLORC has incorporated the worst of all four political *-isms* as the basis for running the country.

The array of accusations of human-rights abuses constantly hurled at the SLORC—such as summary executions, racial discrimination, forced labor, forced relocations, confiscation of property, and arbitrary imprisonment without trial, as well as corruption within the government itself, including kickbacks and payoffs, and laundering drug money—could be interpreted as concrete evidence that pragmatic politics under the guise of economic reform have, in fact, replaced any abstract notion of the political left and right. In fact, there are several survivors of some of these practices who have told the *Special Rapporteur* from the United Nations Commission on Human Rights that Burma could be judged as a microcosm of every repressive and unscrupulous system of government throughout history: the Gulags in Soviet Russia because of the widespread practices of forced labor, especially among the ethnic minorities; the Nazis in Germany because of the persecution of religious minorities such as the Rohingya Muslims, who fled to Bangladesh in 1992 because of forced relocations and extrajudicial killings perpetrated by the government; the Dirty War in Argentina because of the many students and other civilians who simply disappear, or who are imprisoned and tortured; and the nineteenth- and early-twentieth-century British and French colonial period throughout Africa and the Far East because of the class system within the country that subjugates the poor or powerless for the benefit of the rich and powerful.

Under the Ne Win regime, the country's flirtation with socialism was described as The Burmese Way to Socialism. Currently, as the SLORC purports to be moving toward capitalism, the regime refers to its version of that system as The Burmese Way to Capitalism.

In the hierarchy of the Burmese military, the soldiers who graduate from the Defense Service Academy, or DSA, the Burmese equivalent of West Point, consider themselves superior to those military men who attended Officers' Training School, or OTS.

These two very separate and closed "fraternities" are not based only on social nuance, but also on intellectual prowess. Those who attend OTS are accepted after completing only the equivalent of tenth grade, and are required to spend only six months before graduating with the rank of second lieutenants.

The DSA's entrance requirement is the equivalent of a high school diploma, followed by four years of attendance during which time students take advanced subjects such as military science before graduating as second lieutenants.

The result is that high-ranking soldiers from one school tend to promote only those who have the same scholastic background.

General Khin Nyunt is the product of Officer's Training School. He is not only the most imaginative man in the SLORC, but as Chief of Military Intelligence, he is also the most well-informed leader in the country as well as the most feared. The army considers Military Intelligence, or MI as it is called, or even more correctly, the Directorate of Defense Services Intelligence, or DDSI, to be the military's own "gestapo."

On my first visit to Burma, I conducted a three-hour taped interview with General Khin Nyunt, portions of which were broadcast on Fox Television Network in the United States, and published in French in the quarterly review *Politique Internationale*.

My impression was that General Khin Nyunt was extremely brilliant, with an uncanny ability to retain the most minute detail. Married to a physician and the father of two sons, Khin Nyunt is an astute micromanager and a workaholic who often sleeps in his office, not returning home for weeks. Those who work with him claim that he is a man without any vices. In his spare time, he enjoys reading his vast collection of secret files that he has compiled on everyone in the country, including foreigners who report on or do business with the SLORC. Like any powerful dictator, General Khin Nyunt has his own list of enemies.

A small man with a compact body, horn-rimmed glasses, and a wandering left eye, Khin Nyunt has an interesting way of standing loosely, hands dangling at his sides, shifting from one foot to the other, almost like a boxer circling his opponent in the ring. There is something curiously feminine about his soft graceful hands with his cluster ring of rubies, emeralds, sapphires, and a center diamond, which he wears on his right ring finger. His nails are well groomed, and the skin on his face is unblemished and smooth. When he greeted me, he shook my hand firmly, and spoke in a tone of voice that was direct, calm, and pleasant. Several times during our meeting, I had the impression that he regarded me as a misinformed child concerning what he judged were my preconceived and false notions of Burma. "The Myanmar people have different customs, habits, and practices than you in the West," he admonished me gently. During other moments of our three hours together, I felt that he expected me to write favorably about the SLORC, in return for the regime's unusual courtesy and cooperation that they had extended me. "When I first saw you, I felt that you were different than the others," General Khin Nyunt told me. "I believe you will report fairly on our country, and the good work that the SLORC has done for the people." Portions of my interview with General Khin Nyunt follow.

*   *   *

BV: After Aung San Suu Kyi's party, the National League for Democracy, won the majority of the vote in the 1990 elections, why did you refuse to relinquish power?

General Khin Nyunt: When we first assumed responsibility in 1988, the situation was unimaginable. The country was on the verge of chaos and anarchy, which was the reason the armed forces assumed responsibility, to prevent the country from slipping into disintegration. Since that time we have been trying our best to build up our country to have a firm foundation of economic development in accordance with our aims. We also look at our situation in terms of geopolitics since our neighbors are two of the most populous nations in the world—China and India. Our government has spent a lot of money for the development of border areas, trying to dispel mistrust and suspicion of the national races by raising their standard of living. We are also taking measures to eradicate opium by crop substitution. While we are implementing the necessary reforms in the political system, we are also introducing a new economic system, and although our country has natural resources, we are lagging behind in capital as well as in technology.

BV: How are you managing without outside aid, especially since you claim to be eradicating poppy growth, which brings tremendous revenues?

General Khin Nyunt: It is true that we receive no loans from the World Bank, the IMF or even from western countries, which means in order to get the necessary funds, we have to depend on our agriculture and introduce double and triple cropping to develop our natural resources. As far as opium is concerned, it was never our people who got rich from poppy, it was always the brokers from across the border that profited. Currently, we are inviting foreign investors from abroad and although we have been successful to a certain extent, if we don't get more investment and aid the country will suffer. We are also trying to have economic development, building infrastructure projects like bridges across the Irawaddy River, dams all over the country and reservoirs. The previous estimate for these projects was about $100 million, but because we work on our own, we were able to do it for $10 million.

BV: There have been many accusations that your government denies people basic human-rights. How do you respond to those accusations?

General Khin Nyunt: Although our government is in the form of a military government or military junta, we are not suppressing the people. We are trying our best as an interim government to achieve political stability and economic development as well as bring about improvement in the social sphere. We are trying to follow the example set by General Aung San, to implement in practical ways his words.

BV: What about specific accusations such as forced labor and forced relocations of the population?

General Khin Nyunt: People who have not been to the country have an impression that we are brutal and cruel, they regard us as oppressive, as if we are ruling the country by force, as if there is no human-rights in the country. Why such a perception? This is essentially because the information they get is through the media and also because the information they get is not directly from us, the source is from third parties and as you know, there are groups even in your country, in New York, Los Angeles, and Washington, who are against us and the information they are providing cannot be positive to us. Another source of wrong information is the armed groups operating along the border with Thailand and these groups are also generating wrong information as part of their activities.

BV: Not only did your government ignore the election results and refuse to allow Aung San Suu Kyi to lead the country, but you also put her under house arrest for six years and still continue to arrest members of her party. How do you justify your actions?

General Khin Nyunt: Regrettably we find that Aung San's daughter, Aung San Suu Kyi, is making efforts to derail our efforts, by launching a campaign against us together with people who are trying to create problems in our country. She is trying her best to hinder our progress. If she were to try to make our work successful, it would be best for everybody, but unfortunately she is not doing that. As I have mentioned, we love and respect Aung San and since Suu Kyi is the daughter of Aung San, we also have a special attachment to her since she is the daughter of our national hero. Because she did not lead a normal life, in accordance with our religious teachings and customs and traditions, we feel we have to look after her and care for her. Unfortunately she is not leading a normal life of a normal citizen because she is trying to cause political confusion and instability and unrest when at the moment we have peace and tranquility in the country. Although we love and respect her father, it is very difficult for us to have the same feelings for her because of her actions.

BV: You call yourself an interim government, and have indicated that when representatives to the national convention complete a new constitution, you will step down. When will that be?

General Khin Nyunt: We have to take into consideration the special features of our nation, the fact that we have many different nationalities and the problem of armed insurgency, and also the strategic position of our country with two of the most populous countries—India and China—as our neighbors. That is why we called for a national convention to draft a new constitution, a convention with representatives from all the national races and different strata of society. When we started in 1993, we had 700 representatives, and now we have 135 different national races in the country, which means we must have a consensus in the national convention among these races. We assumed responsibility in 1988, and in 1989 we started to invite the various armed races to return to the legal fold. I went into the jungle and secretly met and engaged in complicated and tense discussions with all these representatives from these armed groups. It wasn't an easy task to convince them to return to the legal fold but one by one these armed groups have returned. You can appreciate how delicate this situation is. If our actions are wrong there will be armed uprisings all over the country, which means all our actions have to be the right moves. Some of these groups are already participating in the national convention, and even if they cannot get all of their demands, if we don't handle it correctly, they can pose a great danger to the country. We have to supply them with rice and other supplies, and we have to look after their other needs, and only the army can handle the situation or these groups will go back to the jungle and begin fighting all over again. It is not possible to give a timetable to finish the national convention to have a new constitution. We must have enough time to reach consensus until everyone is satisfied. We are not in a position to say if it will finish in one or two years.

BV: What is your most serious criticism of Aung San Suu Kyi?

General Khin Nyunt: Aung San Suu Kyi was not here for most of her life so naturally she cannot understand all our problems. After her father passed away, she went with her mother at the age of fourteen, when she was appointed Ambassador to India, and later she left for London. From that time she drifted apart from our country and didn't regularly come back to our country. She married an Englishman and settled down and became more apart from the country. If she had come back and worked for the country and married a Myanmar citizen, she may have been able to become a national leader. But when she came back in 1988, at our invitation to care for her ailing mother, the communist party cells saw her as a great advantage because she is the daughter of national hero. They believed that if they could push her into the front and take advantage of her position it would serve their purposes.

BV: Do you believe that the communists are still a threat to Myanmar?

General Khin Nyunt: Our country and people know that communist insurgents have been giving us trouble since time of independence. It is the communists' fault that the country has been lacking in economic development, and even the leaders of insurgent groups have been fighting against the communists. Our armed forces have been fighting them for so long and we do not want to see a communist-dominated government nor do we want communist ideology. The events of 1988 and the communist organizers pushed Suu Kyi as the leader of demonstrations. We were well aware of the dangers to this country caused by this communist conspiracy. Another reason was due to incitement of insurgent groups which resulted, even in the middle of Yangon, of people getting beheaded. This went against the very nature of Buddhist teachings and religion. We are never that cruel or brutal but such things happen among the communists during communist purges. In 1988 the situation became anarchy and Suu Kyi was thrust into the leadership role. All around her there were communists and leftists pushing her to take a more strident stand against the previous government as well as the armed forces. People roamed the streets armed and there was no one to control the situation, not the politicians or Suu Kyi, in fact, politicians began to fade into the background. Because of these conditions, the armed forces had to step in and take responsibility for the nation.

BV: If there is a boycott imposed on Myanmar by the West, how seriously will that affect your government's goals for social and economic progress?

General Khin Nyunt: As you know we are not receiving any foreign assistance from abroad and we have to depend on our own resources. In that case, we have border trade with our neighboring countries, particularly with China and Thailand. As you know, our border with China is over 2,000 kilometers long and similarly with Thailand our border is 2,000 kilometers long and that is why through the border trade we have been able to get necessary commodities needed by the people. Even if there is boycott by western countries, this border trade will meet the needs of our people as an interim measure.

BV: Is your government interested in having better relations with the West?

General Khin Nyunt: We would like to have good relations with everyone, whether or not we receive assistance. We want good relations.

BV: What are your goals for Myanmar?

General Khin Nyunt: We have already made many strides. Our country has 45 million people and we have to look after our social needs as well as our political and economic needs, particularly education. We must also develop the necessary health care facilities for people in the countryside as well as in the cities as well as raising the standards in the universities. In the rural areas, we need to raise the standards of the hospitals so we are doing our best to look after the social needs of the people. Previously in Yangon, there were a lot of squatters around the city, which affected the health and environment of the city. That is why we have built new satellite towns and relocated people from shanty huts to apartment buildings, all to raise the standard of living, which shows the endeavors of the government. But what it shows most is that if the people and the army along with the government are working together, we can achieve these good results. We are not a rich country and only if we work together can we improve the quality of life for our people.

17

THERE ARE sixty-six cabinet members within the Burmese government and of those, 90 percent are military men, including twenty-two high-ranking members of the SLORC who are at the core of the regime, and who serve as directors of various strategic departments within the government. Although all twenty-two SLORC members technically enjoy an equal amount of prerogative, prestige, and privilege, several are more powerful because of their positions within the government. For instance, several non-SLORC generals often have more power than lower-ranking military men who are officially members of the SLORC. Without exception, it is because those non-SLORC military men are in charge of ministries that afford them contacts with foreigners and, therefore, with foreign investment.

General David Abel, a respected economist, is responsible for evaluating every potential foreign investor or international company before any joint venture is approved between them and the SLORC.

General Maung Maung, another well-placed non-SLORC member, is the Secretary of the Foreign Investment Commission, and was the first SLORC member I interviewed on my initial trip to Rangoon. Physically, he resembles a younger and smaller version of Wayne Newton, given his low forehead, square-shaped face, and the way he combs his hair in a 1950s-style pompador.

A religious Buddhist, General Maung Maung is married to a small, bespectacled woman who appears to be kind and intelligent, although she barely speaks when she is in his presence.

Appointed Minister of the Ministry of Livestock and Fisheries in January 1992, the diminutive former fighter pilot in the Burmese Air Force, trained in California, is credited with being the first SLORC member to privatize a major government industry. Until 1988 when the SLORC took power, all businesses and banks throughout Burma were nationalized during the twenty-six year reign of General Ne Win. Unfortunately, General Maung Maung's close friendship and professional involvement with an American businesswoman, Miriam Marshall Segal, cost him his ministry.

Segal, an American of Israeli nationality and Polish parentage, is one of the SLORC's most ardent defenders, going so far as to prove her loyalty to the regime by testifying on several occasions before the United States Congress in an effort to dissuade its members from imposing sanctions on Burma.

Married to a retired heart surgeon who himself has had a heart transplant, and living in New York City, Segal has been involved in Burma for more than twenty years, or as she puts it, "I began the first successful cottage industry in Burma."

Segal's cottage industry developed into more sophisticated ventures, which continue to be profitable. Currently, she has gift stores in several luxury hotels, tries to broker deals between the SLORC and various international companies, and has positioned herself as the best person to know to obtain introductions to the SLORC. During my first trip to Burma, it was Segal who arranged for me to stay in the same guest house with her, which happened to be owned and operated by the DDSI, and who organized several interviews for me with members of the regime. In addition to the proximity of our living arrangements, Segal also attended various official functions to which I had been invited.

Segal is a small and highly vain woman in her sixties, whose collection of creams, wigs, makeup, and Burmese jewelry that she carries back and forth on her many trips takes up most of the room in her suitcases. She keeps a complete separate wardrobe of Burmese *longyis* in a cedar closet at that DDSI hotel in Rangoon. Employing local Burmese to dress her, bathe her, act as her secretary, driver, major domo, companion, trainer, and masseuse, Segal has completely embraced the practices of her friends in the SLORC by paying these people less than what would be the minimum wage anywhere in the world. For example, her Burmese driver, who is on duty eighteen hours a day, is paid a daily rate of $25.00, while her masseuse is paid $3.00 for a one-hour session.

Despite the working conditions, Segal's staff fawn over and pander to her whenever she appears in Rangoon—usually four times a year for two-month visits. Without exception, they consider themselves lucky. Sadly, given the situation in Burma, they are lucky. Not only are they guaranteed a regular salary—more than the average Burmese—but they also get leftover food from expensive restaurants where Segal dines. Even the eggs and toast from Segal's daily hotel breakfast that she doesn't eat are wrapped up in a small refrigerator and doled out to the children of her staff.

The Burmese who form Segal's elite workforce also consider themselves privileged to be so close to the realm of power. Often, a secretary or assistant will accompany her when she makes her rounds of visits to friends such as General Khin Nyunt, General Abel, and General Maung Maung, among others.

One of Segal's favorite expressions is, "It's for the good of the country."

Segal's problems, which ultimately caused General Maung Maung's decline, began during a bitter battle of control over a multinational Burmese prawn-processing venture. At the time, Segal had an exclusive arrangement with Peregrine, a Japanese-owned company, to help establish itself in Burma with the aid and sanction of the SLORC, or more specifically, because of her special relationship with General Maung Maung. In fact, Bertil Lintner, a journalist out of Bangkok for the *Far Eastern Economic*

Review and the author of *Outrage*, published in 1989, in which he attacks the SLORC for its brutal response to the 1988 disturbances, says, "I have a copy of a printed handout where Miriam Marshall Segal states that Peregrine Myanmar, which she ran in Rangoon until she was fired, had unique access to the army's pension funds. And, as everybody knows, these 'funds' are a euphemism for laundered drug money."

Segal was abruptly fired by Peregrine, however, when a series of faxes ended up by mistake in Peregrine's offices, making the company directors aware of Ms. Segal's involvement with one of their most important competitors, Mitsui. What resulted after that was a successful multi-million-dollar lawsuit brought by Peregrine against Segal in a New York court in which they were awarded a $4.9 million judgment against her, which she is currently appealing.

General Maung Maung's involvement in the affair came about during that same trial in New York when several of those faxes were offered as evidence. Apparently, at the time Segal was dismissed by Peregrine, in an effort to avenge herself, she faxed General Maung Maung, suggesting that he use his influence to "plant" incriminating evidence on certain of her business rivals so that the SLORC would have valid reason to throw them out of the country.

After the trial, not only were Segal's assets at risk—including her jewelry, her Central Park West cooperative apartment, her bank accounts, and her Burmese antiques, which she had brought out of the country over the course of a decade and which fill her New York apartment—but also the usually low-profile SLORC found itself implicated in a New York court.

General Maung Maung's illustrious career exporting Burmese prawns and shrimp ended.

The SLORC, however, was kind to General Maung Maung. A loyal military man since graduating from the Defense Service Academy in 1955, he was given another lucrative post by the regime dealing with foreign investors. As for Miriam Marshall Segal and her physician husband, a self-admitted "liberal democrat" who also has become a staunch supporter of the SLORC, the couple is now treated with greater caution and distance by the generals.

It was through Miriam Marshall Segal that I was invited to General Maung Maung's home on the outskirts of Rangoon. On the way there, she cautioned me that his house was nothing particularly lavish, since the general earned only approximately $50 a month. Compared with the thatched roof huts and other slum apartment houses in which the majority of people live, however, General Maung Maung's two-story, ten-room house, while not museum caliber, was certainly luxurious by Burmese standards. As for his meager salary, it is true that officially he earns only that amount. The difference of course is that General Maung Maung, unlike the majority of Burmese who earn even less, has the opportunity to supplement his income.

During a meeting I had with a former government official and current member of the pro-democracy party, I learned how every SLROC official who deals in foreign investment has a "license to steal." "For example," the NLD member began, "suppose the SLORC agrees to sell one million tons of rice at $230 per ton. A memorandum of understanding [MOU] is written by the SLORC to the buyer for a sum of $238 per ton. Sometimes, the kickback is paid in one amount, and sometimes it's paid shipment by shipment."

According to the majority of NLD members with whom I talked, General Khin Nyunt is the only member of the SLORC who does not take bribes or benefit from any money-laundering schemes having to do with drugs or foreign investment. Further, while General Khin Nyunt is a leading advocate of opening up Burma to economic and technological development, his reputation of honesty only augments his power over other SLORC members. According to sources within the government, no one has anything on Khin Nyunt that could disgrace him or cause him his position of power.

In order to separate General Khin Nyunt from the other twenty-one generals of his rank who head various government departments, a special post was created for him called "The Strategic Affairs of the Nation," which in essence puts him in charge of every aspect of Burmese life.

A prominent Burmese who is close to the general explains the reason that General Khin Nyunt has remained so powerful. "It isn't only that he doesn't take bribes," the man told me, "but also because Secretary One—as he is known throughout Burma—refuses to take any initiative on his own or make any unilateral decisions. Any action that Khin Nyunt does take has already been checked out with his colleagues within the SLORC. The result is that he is never blamed for making a wrong decision, and always praised for making the correct one."

During the same interview, the prominent Burmese also said that Secretary One is considered to be fair by his underlings because he does not subscribe to the "old-boy network" of separating soldiers according to whether they are products of OTS or DSA. General Khin Nyunt tries to be impartial when it comes to promoting men or giving favors that result in plum positions within the government.

In Burma, military commanders literally "own" their battalions since they are forced to raise private funds to pay for the care and feeding of the soldiers within their command. Consider the power of a battalion leader who is the only source of food, income, and support for approximately 700 men, all armed with sophisticated weapons. Within the Burmese military, loyalty among the enlisted men toward their superior officers takes on an almost slave-like devotion.

According to the International League for Human Rights in New York, local SLORC commanders in rural and border areas belong to the Law and Order Restoration Council, or LORC, use forced labor usually plucked from many of the rural ethnic villages, and forced donations, squeezed from the poor, to both aid and feed their troops. LORC commanders stationed with their units in rural and border areas require that each village contribute one soldier, or pay a fine of 3,000 kyats or $30 per month, calculated to be the monthly cost of one soldier. Since the average Burmese earns less than that in a month, the consequences for those who are either too old, too young, or too sick to work and, as a result, are required to pay a substitute fine, are dire. Often, the village head will provide the army with the strongest person in the village in order to spare the others.

Senior General Than Shwe, although officially chairman of the SLORC, functions more as a chairman emeritus. As head of state or prime minister, Than Shwe is usually the SLORC member who travels abroad for public relations reasons, promoting Burma as an ideal place for foreign investment. General Than Shwe is also credited with Burma's acceptance into ASEAN, the Association of South East Asian Nations, both as an observer in July 1996, and eventually as a full member in July 1997.

Founded in 1967, ASEAN's original members are Indonesia, Malaysia, the Philippines, Singapore, and Thailand. In 1984, Brunei became the sixth member, and in 1995, Vietnam became the seventh member of ASEAN. In 1987, Laos attained observer status, as did Cambodia in 1995.

Although neither Senior General Than Shwe nor General Khin Nyunt commands and feeds a battalion of soldiers, the two men draw their base of support primarily from their civilian staff as well as from those under their command at military intelligence. Together with General Khin Nyunt, Senior General Than Shwe is in charge of the "war room," an elite group of military men that surpasses the numerical power of the 700 soldiers usually found in a battalion. Regardless of how much dissatisfaction is voiced, or how much grumbling might go on concerning unfair rules and regulations often found within the ranks, when an order comes down from the war room, every soldier from every battalion obeys swiftly and without question.

The power structure of the SLORC does not impinge on the continuing power of General Ne Win. Although the retired dictator is seen only by a select few, and never goes out of his house or attends official functions, many claim that he is still the final word when it comes to every political, financial, defense, and security issue. In fact, it is widely believed throughout Burma that General Ne Win handpicked his successor, General Khin Nyunt.

U Bo Hla Tint, the Finance Minister of the National League for Democracy party whose headquarters-in-exile is in Washington, D.C., has met General Ne Win several times. "After meeting with Ne Win for one hour," U Bo Hla Tint says, "you respect him because he is charismatic. And while he is considered ruthless and power-hungry, in person he can be very charming. He wants nothing more than to be loved by his people."

Today, Ne Win is eighty-six years old and casts a shadow across Burma similar to the shadow cast by Castro, or by Tito or Franco when they were alive. Even now, almost ten years after he officially stepped down, the rumors about him continue.

Some people say that Ne Win is dying of cancer; others claim he has gone insane since relinquishing power; yet others swear he is living a peaceful life with his children and grandchildren. Whatever his emotional condition, General Ne Win, according to most people who either know him or know someone who is close to him, is enormously rich, with bank accounts in Switzerland, holdings on the New York Stock Exchange, investments in Thailand, and interests in several multinational companies in Burma. Married to his fifth wife, Daw Ni Ni Myint an Arakanese (an ethnic minority) woman, he has seven children who are all married with children of their own, and who are all involved in international business ventures, and considered to be the most important people to know if multinational deals are to be made in the country. Although most people have not seen General Ne Win since 1988, there are a few Burmese citizens who claim to be his friend. The person who has the most access to the retired dictator, other than General Khin Nyunt, is his daughter, Sanda, who owns a popular discotheque in Rangoon.

In an interview with Sanda Win, she insisted that her father is in good health, spending most of his time in his vast library where he studies Buddhist sutras and meditates. To control his own destiny, his daughter explained, her father also indulges in a prevalent Burmese practice called *yedayache*, for which he walks backward over a bridge at night, or has his pilot circle his plane nine times over the place of his birth while he is seated in the plane on a wooden horse.

When Ne Win was in power, his circle of friends was extensive both inside and outside of the country. He made frequent trips to the West, often to Vienna where he consulted a psychiatrist by the name of Hans Hoff. According to Dr. Hoff's former nurse, Ingrid Geisler, now retired, Ne Win financed his sessions and his trips by paying with bags of rubies and other precious stones.

In April 1987, Ne Win made his last trip to the United States when he traveled to Oklahoma for a week to visit an American woman named Ardith Dolese. Apparently, the general credited the woman with having saved his life forty years earlier in England when she referred him to her doctor when he was seriously ill. Although Ne Win is considered to be the puppet master of the regime, his photographs have disappeared from billboards, and he never appears in public because he is fearful of assassination. According to sources within the SLORC, there was only one attempt on the general's life.

In 1966, a major in the army, Kyaw Zaw Myint, an Anglo-Burmese, tried to assassinate General Ne Win by poisoning his bottle of Chivas Regal scotch. When the plot failed, Kyaw Zaw Myint ran away, ending up in Australia. In revenge, Ne Win expelled all Anglo-Burmese from the army. This might have cost General David Abel his high position in the military, had it not been for a close associate of the dictator who protected the Anglo-Burmese general. As a result of being the token Anglo in the military, General Abel is forced to watch his every move or all Anglo-Burmese living in Burma will suffer. According to a source in military intelligence, General Abel is ranked among the SLORC members who are considered "basically decent people, even if they are scared of everyone and everything."

According to several political analysts based in Washington, D.C., the United States once categorically supported many military regimes as a means to combat what the Americans considered to be continued communist threats in underdeveloped countries. Now that the Soviet Union has collapsed, those same sources say, the Americans have stopped being tolerant or supportive of repressive military juntas. "We know that we are a military government first," General David Abel admits, "but we also know that the military has given back power to the people three times in its history after it took over during a crisis. This will be the fourth time we have promised to give the people back the responsibility of governing."

General Khin Nyunt, during my interview with him, made it clear that the SLORC will step down only when there is a new constitution. Concerning rumors that Ne Win runs Burma, Khin Nyunt amended, "The people run Burma. The people are writing a new constitution. The people will decide when it is finished and the SLORC is no longer needed."

18

DURING THE LAST WEEK of my visit to Burma, I was invited to meet with four members of the National Convention convening commission. The men—U Aung Khin Tint, the former Auditor General of the Union of Myanmar; Dr. Myo Htun Lynn, legal consultant to the SLORC; U Aye Maung, a lawyer; and Nu Nu Yee, a member of the Union of Myanmar Chamber of Commerce—had been friends since their university days, all graduating in the class of 1949 from the Rangoon Institute of Technology.

Accompanied by Colonel Hla Min, I was driven to a large two-story wood-shingled structure somewhere in Rangoon, situated in the middle of a leafy green park resembling an upscale New England summer resort. When the car pulled up into the circular driveway, lined by perfectly trimmed topiary bushes, my four hosts as well as a half dozen other men, some holding cameras, others clutching notepads and pens, were waiting outside to greet us. As it turned out, the session would be scrupulously recorded and photographed. In fact, later that night the encounter appeared on the Myanmar nightly news.

From the moment the National Convention members led me into the conference room, and invited me, still accompanied by Colonel Hla Min, to sit in the first row of the empty auditorium, I sensed an undercurrent of excitement. Photographers snapped pictures, while waiters wearing white gloves bustled about serv-ing tea and coffee, small sandwiches and pastries. My four hosts, seated in a row on the stage, whispered and smiled as they ar-ranged their papers.

The men began by introducing themselves, each one explain-ing in turn what he had done throughout his professional life, and how he had been retired when the government called him back into service to help draft the country's third constitution.

As the men chatted among themselves, it was obvious they were having a good time. There was a sense of camaraderie and fun that made me think I was visiting a retirement club whose members were about to play checkers, rather than what had been described as an official government committee that was con-tributing to the country's third constitutional process.

It didn't take long for me to understand the SLORC's inge-nuity. The regime had found the perfect way to achieve exactly what they wanted while, at the same time, rewarding loyal citi-zens who had settled into retirement and had no burning moti-vation to change their lives, habits, or country.

Under the SLORC's own rules, when the constitution is writ-ten, they must call democratic elections and relinquish power. It is obviously in the SLORC's best interests to have the National Convention drag on for as long as possible without producing a new constitution. As for the four retirees, they are quite content to meet several times a week to discuss democracy—a stimu-lating subject in the abstract—without having any pressure or precise time frame imposed on them to come to any concrete conclusions.

As if he read my mind, U Aye Maung, one of my hosts, con-firmed my impressions by making the following statement: "We are in no particular rush since we are not here to write a consti-tution but rather to lay down the basic principles for the draft-ing of what will be our country's third constitution."

His colleague, Nu Nu Yee, smiled and added, "We consider ourselves a think tank since it is not necessary for us to vote on

anything, but rather just discuss the overview and general out-
line to be included in the constitution at some point."

In case I didn't understand their duties, or grasp the importance of the whole constitutional exercise, Dr. Myo Htun Lynn,
seated to Nu Nu Yee's left, offered his opinion, which was punc-
tuated by his colleagues' laughter and heads bobbing up and
down emphatically. "We are holding a national convention although we are fortunate not to have any time limit and not to be
under any duress to finish. Elections will take place only after the
new constitution is completed."

"When is that?" I asked.

"After the adoption of the constitution, elections will be held
[laughter]. You see, in the western media there has been much
confusion since people believe what Aung San Suu Kyi has told
them, that elections in 1990 were to choose leaders. The truth is
that elections were to choose representatives to draft a constitution. And, as secretary of the elections, you will see my name
more than a thousand times, so I know what I am saying [ap-
plause, heads bobbing up and down]."

I asked what the SLORC's objective was when they took
power in 1988.

"First of all, the mandate to have a multiparty democracy was
issued by the SLORC on September 18, 1988. When the SLORC
took power, its main objective was to restore law and order. The
second objective was to have good communication, and the
third objective was the welfare of the public. All along, there was
never any doubt that only after these three objectives were met
would there be multiparty elections. After the 1988 disturbances
when the people clamored for these multiparty elections, the
SLORC said if those three conditions were fulfilled, it would
hold multiparty elections and move toward free-market economy. In 1990, it did hold multiparty elections but the question
remains—and you are well-educated—can a country govern in
a multiparty system without a constitution? The answer is no.
A ship without a rudder cannot reach its destination just as a
country without a constitution cannot achieve its aims. You see,

perhaps there was confusion because the last constitution, written in 1974, stipulates there will be only one party, the Myanmar socialist party, and that was a one-man show [laughter]."

This wasn't the first time in Burmese history that a dictator or group of dictators attempted to fool the country and the world. In 1974, a huge trade deficit and internal political strife forced the government under General Ne Win to introduce so-called political and economic reforms. As a result, a second constitution was drafted that allowed all political power to remain with Ne Win while at the same time creating the illusion that there were new reforms.

I asked, if the SLORC convened a national convention in January 1993 to draw up a new constitution, why they handpicked the delegates and controlled the proceedings so that any opposition views would be ignored.

"The western world is confusing national politics with party politics," Colonel Hla Min interrupted.

I asked if the SLORC had instructed those people who are participating in the National Convention to draft a constitution that would guarantee a dominant role for the military.

"What we are trying to say is that the military should have a role when it comes to national affairs but when we say national politics we mean national affairs," Colonel Hla Min continued. "In the past, we in the military didn't have this role. This meant that we were always at the barracks until the politicians messed up and then we were called out of the barracks and ordered to solve the problem. When we say that we were brought out to solve the problem, the politicians wanted a military solution, which means that we risk our lives. In some cases the government was wrong, but we had no choice. We had to fight and we did this for forty-five years. This time we [the military] said 'No!' We wanted to be involved in the decision making."

I wondered if it was the SLORC's intention to base the new constitution on the Indonesian tradition since the SLORC has always been attracted to the Indonesian concept of *dwifungsi*, or dual function, which gives the armed forces an institutionalized role in political life.

"Burma has always considered that it shares military traditions with Indonesia. Not only did both countries struggle to win independence from colonial masters, but both nations had to deal with rebellions from within that threatened their national unity. The SLORC wants a military regime that would be assured of a role in the evolution of the country toward a more democratic system of government, by participating in the national leadership of the future state government."

I commented that for the SLORC to achieve that goal in a democratic way, it seems imperative for them to have a dialogue with Aung San Suu Kyi and the NLD. After all, the NLD did win the elections in 1990.

"In late 1994 and throughout the following year, the SLORC leadership met with Aung San Suu Kyi on two occasions."

I pointed out that on both occasions, the SLORC refused Aung San Suu Kyi's request to have a dialogue on the country's political future. Why was that?

"The reason the SLORC has refused to negotiate with The Lady or with other members of the NLD is because for now, the constitution is more vital to the interests of all Myanmar citizens, including the various ethnic minorities, than agreeing to disagree with the NLD."

I asked why the SLORC has refused to make some kind of a timetable to finish drafting the constitution.

"The reason we have no fixed schedule to finish this constitution is because this convention is based on consensus while our previous constitutions were based on referendum. There's a big difference. The other way was not democratic because the majority in our country (70 percent) are Burmans. If we based the new constitution on referendum the minorities wouldn't have much say, and we don't believe this is fair. Now the minorities may be small in number but they have a big voice, which makes it very difficult to reach consensus. For the first time in our history, we are giving priority to minorities. It has taken more time than expected but if things turn out in the direction we plan, the outcome will be very good because this will be the constitution that will include all the 135 nationalities and subnationalities."

The issue of the ethnic minorities, including the problem of those groups that had not come back into the "legal fold," was also discussed by the members of the National Convention. Aung Khin Tint offered the following opinion. "The issues have been properly thrashed out so that even the smallest minority will be heard," he began. "Now, while we [the Burmans] won the largest number of seats, we are going on the basis of consensus, and while people say we're going slowly, a full-fledged democracy takes time. Actually, the NLD themselves are putting so many obstacles in our way, saying this is wrong, or that is wrong, that in the end they are making it difficult to ever achieve a consensus. What we have told the NLD is that we will deal with their issues in the next session, since the most important factor is that sixteen groups have put down their arms and come back into the legal fold. The understanding is that the people who came back before 1993 are already in the National Convention—something like eight groups are there—but the seven groups that came in after 1993—a big group like the Kachin group for example—are not there. I think the Kachins have agreed that if they can, they will participate but the rules are such that it is difficult to accommodate latecomers. Still, the Kachins have sent a number of groups to the convention to study what has been done and to transmit their views. At the moment, the groups that made cease-fire agreements with the SLORC are keeping their arms because the agreement was not a surrender, it was an accommodation. But as soon as the constitution is put into place, these groups must surrender their arms. Constitution timing must be such so that these groups have properly adjusted to the new surroundings and can solve their problems with each other so all the minority groups can put down their arms."

A summary of Aung Khin Tint's position is that, on the basis of the cease-fire agreements the SLORC has entered into with approximately sixteen ethnic minorities, the regime claims that a new constitution is needed in order to provide equal rights for all nationalities and minority groups, which would guarantee them an equal say in the government.

During my earlier three-hour meeting with General Khin Nyunt, the leading spokesman of the SLORC, he had already stated what I was told by the four members of the convening committee.

While the SLORC constantly applauds its own achievement of making cease-fire agreements with sixteen ethnic minorities, it neglects to mention that the army continues to wage civil war against other ethnic groups, as well as to engage in massive relocations and forced labor of the majority of the ethnic civilian population.

For instance, as of this writing, the SLORC does not have a cease-fire agreement with the Karen National Union, or KNU, and in a few areas where the SLORC claims to have cease-fires, there is still fighting.

Recent reports have indicated that there is armed conflict not only in the Karen and Kayah states, but also with the insurgent forces in the Shan State, the center of Burma's drug trade, as well as in the Chin State.

According to David Young of the United States Department of State, in terms of human-rights problems in those areas, there are still eyewitness reports of forced labor and forced porterage involving entire villages that are made to work on construction projects or made to carry materials into war zones by the SLORC army. "Obviously, there are still horrible human-rights violations," Young claims, "although recently SLORC has been pressed on that by the international community and by international business so they have started to curtail that a little bit. Reports also indicate that treatment of local people is better if American or other foreign companies are there. The reason is because we have a strong human-rights lobby and there're lots of NGOs (non-government organizations) under pressure from stockholders, which makes them generally more accountable than a company from a country where there are no human-rights groups. In fact, many foreign companies claim that they have a marginal influence on the SLORC. But obviously, it's not enough to stop those practices completely."

Just as disturbing is that those cease-fire agreements fail to address the ethnic nationalities' demands for political autonomy under a federal rather than a centralized system of government. One of the most difficult negotiating points between the SLORC and the various ethnic groups was and is the question of when the minorities would relinquish their arms.

General Khin Nyunt came up with the idea of allowing the sixteen groups to keep their arms until the constitution was drafted. Officially, the rationale was a symbol of good faith and security, as well as a symbol of the intention to create parity between all the ethnic groups who had a long history of war and violence against the central government. There is no doubt that this particular accommodation is the main reason why the SLORC is the first administration in Burmese history that has managed to achieve cease-fires.

During my meeting with the four retirees, U Aung Khin Tint, the former Auditor General of the Union of Myanmar, discussed the fact that the 700 SLORC-appointed participants in the convention are chosen from every social, economic, and political stratum of life in Burma. "Members come from the peasant group, farmers, working class, intelligentsia," U Aung Khin Tint said proudly, "such as university professors, and service personnel including bureaucrats from the ministries, as well as special invited guests. As it stands now, the NLD is the only political party that has refused to participate. They were with us for more than three years, beginning in 1993, and then in November 1995 [laughter] they walked out."

There was one question that the four men refused to address. If the 1990 elections were *not* to choose leaders, but rather to choose representatives to the National Convention, why are the majority of delegates to the National Convention SLORC-appointed and *not* NLD pro-democracy representatives?

It is a question that the SLORC cannot answer.

Given the NLD's definitive majority in the 1990 elections, when the SLORC refused to hand over power, the next best accommodation would have been that the pro-democracy party would be at least given a majority of seats in the National Convention. Yet, out of 677 seats, the NLD was allowed only 86. As a result, in November 1995 Daw Suu Kyi ordered her delegates to walk out of the convention in protest against the way it was progressing, and because elected representatives continued to be underrepresented while SLORC-appointed delegates were clearly in the majority.

In response, the SLORC issued a statement that, based on a technicality in the bylaws of the convention, more than a three-day absence by any individual or party without permission from the military government would result in expulsion.

As it turned out, the NLD walkout at the National Convention provoked a threat issued by General Khin Nyunt that Daw Suu Kyi and her colleagues would be "annihilated" if they tried to destablilize the country. "Adopted sons and daughters of the colonialists under external influence," General Khin Nyunt began, "who are attempting to cause the disintegration of the union and the loss of independence will be annihilated." Although Suu Kyi was not directly named in the general's speech, the words were clearly aimed at her.

General Khin Nyunt's open threat was highly unusual, since most press attacks against Aung San Suu Kyi are made either anonymously or written in the state-controlled press, signed by reviled historical figures known for their treasonous activities.

Following the walkout, NLD leaders announced that the boycott of the National Convention would last "until such time as a dialogue is held on national reconciliation, a genuine multiparty democracy system, and the drafting of a constitution which is supported by the people." Daw Suu Kyi reiterated that "at the moment the NLD has only said that they will not be attending the convention until such time as a proper dialogue has been successfully achieved. . . . It would be regrettable and sad, indeed, if elections had been held in 1990 to hoodwink the people of Burma and the world."

When there was no response from the SLORC concerning a dialogue, Aung San Suu Kyi announced in May 1996 that her party would draw up its own draft of a constitution. Convening a three-day party conference, Daw Suu Kyi took the most dramatic position against the junta she had taken since her release from house arrest the previous July. By taking her battle into the constitutional arena it allowed her a long-term vehicle to build on the NLD election victory. Even an alternative constitution that had no hope of ever being enforced would provide the Burmese people with a clear contrast between a system emphasizing democracy and human-rights and one that was weighted toward a military regime. Asked how ordinary Burmese armed only with courage could prevail against the military, Daw Suu Kyi replied, "That's exactly why there will be change because all they [the SLORC] have is guns. They regard everything we do as confrontational but there's nothing in the law that says you have no right to draft a constitution."

With Burmese music playing in the background, Aung San Suu Kyi closed the session of her party congress by reading resolutions adopted by those eighteen delegates to the NLD convention who had managed to escape arrest and attend. The resolutions demanded the immediate release of all detainees by the SLORC, called for the convening of parliament and a dialogue with the junta, and stated that only elected representatives from the military could sit in parliament, and only under civilian control.

The NLD resolution further stated that the military was "a necessary institution" that should become an "honorable one by sticking to national defense and helping bring about democracy."

Without delay, the SLORC proclaimed a new law forbidding any alternative convention for the purpose of drafting a constitution. Penalties for such activities, the SLORC announced, would result in prison sentences that could range anywhere from five to twenty years. Within days, more than 273 officials from the National League for Democracy Party were arrested in what the government termed as a "preventative effort to stop them from participating in the alternative convention."

Although many were released within a few weeks, Daw Suu Kyi's cousin, U Aye Win, and another close aide were detained and given harsh prison sentences. One of her personal assistants, who had vanished on 13 June while on the way to a local video shop, eventually turned up in Insein Prison.

Nine days later, Daw Suu Kyi's godfather, Leo Nicols, a former honorary consul for Norway, Sweden, Denmark, Switzerland, and Finland, who had been using his fax machine at his home to send Daw Suu Kyi's regular column, "Letter from Burma," to Japan's *Manichi Shimbun* newspaper, was arrested. Charged with possession of an illegal fax machine, Leo Nicols was sentenced to three years in Insein Prison. Two and a half months later, Nicols was dead, the victim of an apparent heart attack. Authorities refused to release his body to his family for an autopsy and instead buried him within twenty-seven hours of his death.

Up until now, the SLORC has not hesitated to use harsh measures to enforce the strict rules governing the National Convention. Recently an NLD delegate, Aung Khin Sint, was sentenced to twenty years in prison for allegedly publishing leaflets critical of the junta's role in the National Convention.

Since the arrest of so many of her colleagues, Daw Suu Kyi has remained circumspect about calling for an alternative convention, although she insists that she is still keeping her options open. "The NLD members may well continue to take part in the government's convention," Daw Suu Kyi says. "Otherwise our voice will not be heard." Yet her two closest associates, U Tin U and U Kyi Maung, both argue that the SLORC-organized convention is an "unacceptable" forum for participation by the NLD. "When we come to the end of our patience, we will let them know," U Kyi Maung says.

In November 1996, in perhaps the most telling statement that the SLORC ever made, General Khin Nyunt announced that with "ten political parties and many indigenous groups returning to the legal fold, it has become necessary . . . to develop principles and procedures to avoid extremes in flexibility in order to ensure the development of the genuine multiparty system we aspire to. No one disputes or dislikes our goal, which is the emergence of a democratic nation. But while we may have a common goal, *we must avoid the mistake of being too earnest about reaching that goal.*"

In late November 1996, twenty-three senior Burmese independence leaders and politicians signed a letter urging the SLORC and the National League for Democracy to hold a dialogue "for the sake of the people and the country." In response, the SLORC branded the twenty-three elders speaking for independence "stooges." Also in late November, several student factions in Rangoon made an appeal to the SLORC chairman, Senior General Than Shwe, and to Aung San Suu Kyi "to strive together for national reconciliation." Pressure on the SLORC to enter into dialogue with pro-democracy activists has also come from various foreign countries as well as from the United Nations General Assembly and the Human Rights Commission. In a written statement submitted to the SLORC, the United Nations General Assembly urged the government to "engage at the earliest possible date in a substantive political dialogue with Aung San Suu Kyi and other political leaders, including representatives of ethnic groups, as the best means of promoting national reconciliation and the full and early restoration of democracy."

On that occasion, the SLORC refused to negotiate with the NLD on the basis of "fairness." "After all," General Khin Nyunt claimed, "there were more than 100 political parties which participated in those elections. How can we meet with one and not the others?"

When eighty-nine of those parties agreed to let Daw Suu Kyi speak as their representative, General Khin Nyunt's response was, "It is unfair. I am representing only one party. Why should I be forced to deal with a coalition of more than eighty parties?"

From then on, the SLORC's response has been consistent, namely that the National Convention is the only forum for dialogue. After the NLD walked out, the entire constitution-drafting process stopped, which made any attempt at reconciliation moot. As of January 1997, the National Convention has resumed, and there have even been rumors that the NLD will rejoin the process. Daw Suu Kyi remains convinced that a dialogue between the NLD and the SLORC is inevitable, and even the SLORC leaves open the possibility. Following the NLD's expulsion from the National Convention, *The New Light of Myanmar* published an editorial that stated, "If Aung San Suu Kyi had remained . . . patient . . . the dialogue she desires so much would have already been in progress. . . . even now she fails to anticipate that the military leadership is well aware of their responsibilities, and may yet be contemplating such a dialogue. Yet, she foolishly goes on to antagonize them with her strident demands and invectives."

During my meeting with the four delegates to the National Convention convening committee, I reminded them that the SLORC keeps insisting they will turn over power and call for new elections only after a constitution is written, and only when there is a "good" government.

I asked them what the definition of "good" is.

One of the delegates replied, "Good is not like the NLD who walked away from us. Let me explain. We were with the NLD until November 1995 and they asked us to have a dialogue. In fact, they wrote us a letter asking us to have a dialogue, which I'm afraid you can't understand because it is in Burmese [laughter]. Anyway, we considered that a dialogue wasn't necessary since we were already having a dialogue in our National Convention. So, they threatened us by saying that if we didn't arrange this dialogue, they would walk out and boycott the National Convention. They didn't attend for two consecutive days, and according to our rules and procedures, any delegate member, without having permission to miss sessions is subject to dismissal. The NLD gave us no alternative but to act according to the rules."

And how much progress has been made so far in drafting this new constitution?

"The constitution already has 104 fundamental points agreed upon, and after another 110 points, it will be completed and put to plebiscite," Nu Nu Yee replied. "It is taking longer than expected but Myanmar has problems that are peculiar to Myanmar. First we have to stabilize the country, and raise the living standards. We cannot talk about politics and democracy unless the people are well-fed and have a good standard of living. Otherwise democracy is a farce. That is a 'good' government. Don't forget this government is a military government. It is not a dictatorship but rather a democracy under military control. The committee of military men governing Myanmar rules sincerely and honestly and has achieved many things. Everyone in Myanmar has to admit that."

*   *   *

In the evening following that meeting, I was taken by a member of the foreign diplomatic corps to visit a prominent professor of history at his home in Rangoon.

The response to my first question—the purpose of the 1990 elections, and why the Burmese people apparently didn't know why or for whom they were voting—was laughter. "Of course the people knew why they were voting," the professor said. "The fact is that the SLORC did make things clear. The people were voting for a new democratic government. The only difference is that the SLORC never expected Aung San Suu Kyi's party to win such an overwhelming majority."

"When she did, the military did the only logical thing when faced with the results—and that was either to cancel the elections, or do something surprisingly more subtle, which was to change the purpose of the elections, which is exactly what happened. Remember, this wasn't the first time in Burma that a regime used an obsolete constitution as an excuse to fool the world. Ne Win did the same thing in 1974, only he did it so the

World Bank and the IMF would loan the country badly needed funds. And it worked because annual loans to Burma grew from around $20 million to $400 million during the 1970s. The next important event that led to this whole farce of drafting a new constitution happened in 1988 when the SLORC dissolved the legislature and other organs of power under the 1974 constitution and proclaimed martial law and, as a consequence, declared that its government was extraconstitutional."

I asked what the purpose of the 700 SLORC-appointed members of the National Convention is.

He replied, "Simply to entrench the army in power, and to make it as hard as possible for the NLD to repeat its electoral triumph of 1990, when it won 80 percent of the vote. Don't forget, in the present constitution, there are two choices. One is that the military will have 25 percent of the seats in the parliament, which means that the military will also have a voice in national affairs, and another clause which states that the military will take a leading role in national politics. But, when the SLORC is confronted with these facts, they differentiate between national affairs and national politics, and that's just ridiculous!"

Concerning the NLD's attempt to draft an alternative constitution, the professor maintained that the idea had met with such forceful resistance and harsh measures by the SLORC that the NLD has since toned down its announcement to challenge the National Convention.

"If the junta thinks they are marginalizing Suu Kyi," the professor explained, "they will probably just continue with low-level harassment of the opposition. But if she seems to be making advances they'll have no compunction about cracking down hard. After the death of Leo Nicols, which touched Suu Kyi deeply, and the arrest and incarceration of so many of her political colleagues, the decision was made by the NLD to keep a low profile for a while."

During the March/April 1996 United Nations Commission on Human Rights held in Geneva, Switzerland, the Commission issued a statement in which they "deplored the harsh sentences meted out to members of political parties and other individuals including persons voicing dissent in regard to the procedures of the National Convention and persons condemned in particular for seeking to meet the *Special Rapporteur* and for having peacefully exercised their right to freedom of expression, movement, and association."

The Commission further "noted with concern that most of the representatives democratically elected in 1990 had been excluded from participating in the National Convention," and that "severe restrictions had been imposed on delegates including members of the NLD who had withdrawn and subsequently were excluded and prevented from meeting or distributing their literature ... [and] that the National Convention does not appear to constitute the necessary steps toward the restoration of democracy."

Although it is certain that the SLORC intends to delay the completion of a new constitution for as long as possible, according to the professor, there are nonetheless justifiable reasons why the operation risks being so lengthy. "As it stands now," the professor said, "the entire process could well take up to ten years. The country desperately needs an infrastructure, cars, buses, and even decent barracks to house the military. Suu Kyi is willing to accept a certain amount of years to accomplish the building of the country from a third-world power, and she is also willing to relinquish the title of head of state, but never at the expense of not bringing democracy to Burma."

It is interesting to note that Daw Suu Kyi is not categorically against some participation by the military. She has qualified her position, however, by stating that any formal role of the military should not be written into the constitution without first putting the question to a vote.

"It was obviously not the sort of thing that we were working for when we started the movement for democracy," Daw Suu Kyi says. "But while this was not our aim when we started our working movement for democracy, everything is open to negotiation and all problems can be solved through goodwill and compromise. As long as all of us wish only for the good of the nation, we should have no trouble."

As it stands today, the NLD's options are limited. The Burmese people still remember the events of 1988 that followed the SLORC's seizure of power after months of pro-democracy demonstrations. Only a very small portion of the population is willing to risk another bout of the violence and anarchy that cost so many lives.

When it comes to the timing of the constitution, the SLORC also faces a dilemma. If the regime gives the slightest encouragement to Aung San Suu Kyi and the NLD, they risk unleashing forces they cannot control. But if the regime continues to ignore The Lady, they will remain at least partially an international pariah and at odds with most of the Burmese people.

What the SLORC is counting on is that several of their tangible achievements—such as the cease-fires with the ethnic groups, as well as the $2 billion in foreign investment that they have attracted—will ultimately convince the people that a SLORC-dominated party is the best solution for the country. When they are secure, and after the new constitution is drafted, the regime will call for elections and once again hope that they win the majority of popular support. If they don't, the outcome could be anything from violence to fear to apathy on the part of the people.

As I was leaving the professor's home that evening, he offered these thoughts. "The sixteen ethnic groups are not anxious to turn over their arms—that is clear—and the SLORC is not anxious to finish drafting the constitution. All this means is that instead of the various groups following the timing of the constitution to disarm, I suspect the SLORC will allow the constitutional process to end only when the minorities are given enough monetary incentive to consider armed struggle a nonlucrative waste of time. By then, the SLORC is hoping that Suu Kyi will have given up, and the other opposition parties will see how the economy is booming and no longer challenge the military regime. When that happens, the SLORC will already have written a new constitution that provides legally for their retaining power."

On my way back to my hotel, I couldn't help remembering something Colonel Hla Min had said that afternoon. "Be logical," he cautioned. "If the SLORC really wanted to declare the election invalid, we could have reacted the way the government did in Nigeria or Algeria when they didn't like the results of their elections."

And how was that?

"We could have hanged the winners," Colonel Hla Min replied.

19

SEVERAL DAYS LATER, in a government guest house on the shores of Inya Lake, Colonel Hla Min arranged for me to meet with a group of ethnic leaders and a "former drug lord" to discuss the cease-fires, as well as their reasons for agreeing to stop producing opium. During those meetings, which lasted for several days, Colonel Hla Min also invited Lieutenant Colonel Thane Han and Colonel Kyaw Thein to brief me in their respective areas of expertise.

Lieutenant Colonel Thane Han is in charge of an eleven-year program that the SLORC has named "The Master Plan." Initiated in 1989 with a budget of more than 1.4 billion kyats, or approximately $350 million, its purpose, according to the regime, is to improve the border areas. Precisely, the objectives of this plan are "To develop the economic and social works and roads and communications of the national races at the border areas, in accordance with the aims of the SLORC which are: Non-disintegration of the Union; Non-disintegration of the national solidarity; Perpetuation of the Sovereignty of the State. To cherish and preserve the culture, literature, and customs of the national races; To strengthen the amity among the national races; To eradicate totally the cultivation of poppy plants by establishing economic enterprises; To preserve and maintain the security, prevalence of law and order and regional peace and tranquility of the border areas."

The primary goal of The Master Plan, according to Lieutenant Colonel Thane Han, is to build hospitals and schools to
educate the rural population in areas of health and child care,
birth control, and general job training and to improve the infrastructure. "The only condition we have set down," he explained,
"is that the groups can no longer stay outside of the law. They
must engage only in legal activities."

To achieve these goals, the SLORC claims they have instituted
a "crop substitution" program. What that means is that the
regime subsidizes the income the groups earn from regular crop
farming to match what some of them had previously earned
from poppy cultivation, which they have allegedly stopped.

Colonel Kyaw Thein, also known as "The Poppyman," is one
of the directors of the Central Commission for Drug Abuse, established to organize and implement the eradication of opium
and poppy production throughout the country. To achieve the
goal of crop substitution, The Poppyman explained that it is
necessary to build roads and railroads to facilitate the transport
of legal crops from the farming areas to the cities, and eventually
to the seaport in Rangoon for export. "Growing poppy was
much easier for the people because the buyers came to them,"
Colonel Kyaw Thein elaborated. "Now, if they're going to grow
other crops, they need an infrastructure to transport them out
of their regions so they can realize a living."

According to a report on human-rights practices in Burma,
compiled by the United States Department of State in 1996, to
build the necessary infrastructure, the regional governments in
charge of each area, named the Law and Order Restoration
Council, or LORC, call upon village heads to supply the workforce. "Government investment in the border areas in road, hospital, and school construction has been modest at best," the
report reads, "and economic development of ethnic minority
areas continues to lag, leaving many living at barely subsistence
levels. Since the focus of the hostilities against armed insur-
gencies has been in the border areas where most minorities are
concentrated, those populations have been disproportionately

victimized by the general brutalization associated with the SLORC's activities."

In response to those charges, Colonel Thane Han, who is in charge of The Master Plan, says, "I've been here overseeing the national program for eight years and there has never been a complaint that somebody didn't get paid for work on a project."

When questioned concerning the incentives that the SLORC has offered the ethnic minorities in rural areas to stop growing poppy and instead begin farming less lucrative products, Lieutenant Colonel Thane Han replied, "It is a moral question. The people were never making money from growing poppy; it was always the traffickers and dealers that made money. The groups never promised us they would give up poppy cultivation outright, and we can't insist on that. What they have agreed is to let the government match their income by crop substitution which will take years to achieve, which is why this Master Plan is an eleven-year program."

The ethnic groups that have entered into peace accords with the SLORC are the Myanmar National Democracy Alliance (MNDA) which entered into a cease-fire agreement with the SLORC on March 31, 1989; the Myanmar National Solidarity Party (MNSP) on September 5, 1989; the National Alliance Army Military and Local Administration Committee (Eastern Shan State) on June 30, 1989; Shan State Army (SSA) on September 24, 1989; New Democratic Army (NDA) on December 15, 1989; Kachin Defense Army (KDA) on January 11, 1991; Pa-O National Organization (PNO) on February 18, 1991; Palaung State Liberation Party (PSLP) on April 21, 1991; Kayan National Guards (KNG) on February 27, 1992; Kachin Independence Organization (KIO) on February 24, 1994; Karenni Nationale People's Liberation Front (KNLF) on May 9, 1994; New Mon State Party (NMSP) on June 29, 1995; and the Karenni National Progressive Party (KNPP) on January 6, 1996.

In January 1996, however, the SLORC announced that they had negotiated perhaps their most important cease-fire with Burma's most powerful drug lord, Khun Sa, and his Mong Tai

Army (MTA). According to the SLORC, the notorious drug lord had surrendered unconditionally.

Once vilified by the Burmese government, Khun Sa is currently living quietly in a luxurious villa in Rangoon under government protection, with nearly a billion dollars stashed away in Switzerland and Thailand. Sources in Rangoon told me that the SLORC allowed Khun Sa to buy and run the public transportation system throughout Rangoon, as well as to invest in several lucrative hotel ventures in partnership with the regime and a group of foreign investors.

According to The Poppyman, Colonel Kyaw Thein, the SLORC allowed Khun Sa to escape prosecution, as well as assured him protection from extradition to the United States where there are several outstanding warrants for his arrest.

"The United States wanted us to turn over Khun Sa because he is a walking encyclopedia," Colonel Kyaw Thein explained. "He knows the name of every major drug dealer in the world, the routes the drugs take, and the amount of production as well as prices the drugs will get on the streets. We decided not to comply with the request by the United States because we were the ones who negotiated the cease-fire with Khun Sa, and we were the ones who lost more than 1,000 men during the fighting. Another reason we refused to turn over Khun Sa is because we don't have an extradition agreement with the United States."

Hasn't the United States supplied Burma with arms and other technical equipment to eradicate poppy?

"In the past, yes. Since 1988, the United States has been diminishing its financial aid to help us solve a problem which is mostly their problem, since heroin is a bigger menace on the streets of America than here in Burma. But more than that, the United States hindered our military operation against Khun Sa when they put an arms embargo on Myanmar. We lost many men because Khun Sa's army was better equipped. Khun Sa had 20,000 men and the terrain over there is very rough."

Asked why the SLORC decided not to put Khun Sa on trial, The Poppyman said, "It's very simple. We managed to solve the problem which is like two teams playing soccer. Suppose one team wins without any assistance or help, that means they can display the trophy anywhere they choose. For us, it is the same thing. This is our success and we are in a position to display our trophy anywhere we like."

According to Colonel Kyaw Thein, the United States did more to try and thwart the SLORC's efforts to sign a peace treaty with Khun Sa than just implementing an arms embargo.

"Three years ago," Colonel Kyaw Thein maintained, "Peter Borne, the former drug czar under the Carter administration, had a secret meeting with Khun Sa. Now, the only reason Khun Sa agreed to meet with Mr. Borne is because he knew what he once did for President Carter, although when he met with him, Mr. Borne was a private citizen. It was out of respect. Khun Sa told us that Mr. Borne offered him arms and money to continue fighting us, and encouraged Khun San to declare himself the president of an independent nation."

Why would Peter Borne encourage Khun Sa to set up an independent nation?

"We believe that the United States sent Peter Borne to try and convince Khun Sa to keep fighting us in the hope that Khun Sa's army would win and our government would topple. Of course, Khun Sa refused the offer when Mr. Peter Borne said that he could not guarantee that the United States government would grant him amnesty. Actually, Khun Sa believed us more when we promised to protect him from extradition to the United States than he believed Mr. Borne or the United States government, especially after what happened to Mr. Noriega."

Why would Khun Sa suddenly decide to give up what was a multi-billion dollar drug business?

"He is sixty-four years old and has about $600 million. I think he just wanted to make peace with himself, and become a true and good Buddhist."

Colonel Hla Min announced that an important former drug lord from the Shan State, who had entered into a cease-fire agreement with the SLORC, would be arriving at the government guest house to explain his reasons for coming back into the legal fold.

The man arrived within a half an hour. Clean shaven and devoid of wrinkles, he appeared to be in his late fifties. Built compactly with muscular arms and a large torso, he entered the room followed by six men who were dressed in *longyis*. The former drug lord shook hands warmly with Colonel Hla Min and Colonel Kyaw Thein. When he shook hands with me, I noticed the heavy gold Rolex watch that he wore on his left wrist. Seated on a sofa next to him, I was told that the former drug lord wanted to make a statement before any questions were asked. As the cameras turned, he began.

"We had been fighting the central government for the last thirty years and in 1996 there were changes in the policy when the military took over the state power. It seemed to us that the new military government was reasonable and practical and it was time to work together with the government to rebuild the nation."

I asked him what made the SLORC's offer different than all the other regimes since Burma won its independence from the British.

"Once we believed that the only way to get equal rights was by fighting. With this government, they are offering us economic incentives to improve our life and our infrastructure. This government makes no false pretense about being a democratic government, and we understand and agree with that. After all, this is the time to bring people together, to adjust and to be tranquil. We have come back into the legal fold because we see with our own eyes what the government says is true. Once this new constitution comes into the picture, many of the ethnic groups will turn over their arms. Don't forget they are not holding onto the arms because they are threatened by the government, but because it is a kind of gentlemen's agreement, a symbolic gesture."

What about opium production? Was it still being grown?

The man smiled and reached into his pocket for several photographs. He offered them to me. There was the same man, dressed in army fatigues and cap seated, next to a westerner, surrounded by other Burmese, some in uniform, some in civilian clothes. Colonel Hla Min introduced us. "You are talking to Khun Sa," he said with obvious pride. After shaking his hand and expressing surprise, I asked, "Who is the man in the photographs with you?"

Always through his interpreter, Khun Sa responded, "Peter Borne. You see, opium was beginning to affect the Myanmar people. There were many drug addicts throughout the country and I understood that much of the blame was on me. Also, many of the drug profits went to buy bullets that killed Myanmar soldiers. It was time to stop and do other things. In the beginning I felt no responsibility for anything that happened with the drugs in the United States since it was the American CIA who provided heroin in the 1950s to finance the Kuomintang troops that invaded parts of Myanmar. At the time, their goal was to stage attacks against the People's Republic of China. Now, I have retired, and I have many assets that were not given to me by the government, but were accumulated during my years of growing poppy. I am an old man." He smiled again. "The drug problem is not on my head."

Asked if, when Peter Borne allegedly asked him to resist the SLORC and declare an independent state, he ever considered that possibility, Khun Sa replied, "Never! The whole problem of heroin around the Golden Triangle was part of a western policy to contain communism. When Peter Borne approached me, he was not prepared to give me any guarantee that I would not face trial in the United States."

When asked if he was on good terms with the SLORC, Khun Sa smiled broadly. "Very good terms. I am helping the country become more developed, while the government is helping my people to have a better life."

I asked him, "Who is the most dangerous enemy of the SLORC?"

"The Mujahid Forces from the Bangladesh-Myanmar border are making alliances with three rebel groups in Arakan, the Myanmar province that borders southeastern Bangladesh. Those are the real enemies because they can draw support from many countries in that region."

At the end of the interview, before Khun Sa was taken away in a nondescript car, followed by an unmarked sedan filled with what were certainly his bodyguards, I asked, "Why have certain SLORC members had meetings with Saddam Hussein?"

Again, Khun Sa smiled. "I am not in the government so I don't know. But, if that is true, the problem of the radical Muslim fundamentalists is not only our problem."

Months later I would learn that not only was Khun Sa heavily invested in real estate and transportation, but he was also selling off some of his assets through other channels. According to a source close to the NLD in Rangoon, one of Khun Sa's sons, Chao Cham Huang, has been charged with the responsibility of selling a 200-ton piece of jade. Currently bids are coming in from Taiwan to the Middle East. According to that same source, the stone is hidden in the Shan State near the Mongkut mine site where it was originally found.

Spend any time in Burma and you realize that amnesia has become a way of life.

20

DONALD KEYSER, the director of the Office of Asia, Africa, Europe, and Multilateral Programs at the Bureau of International Narcotics and Law Enforcement, United States Department of State, believes that the SLORC genuinely wants to keep the country united in order to build it up economically. "The big problem that Burma has is China. While China is Burma's major arms supplier," Keyser contends, "the Burmese military has always considered China [to be] the country's biggest threat in terms of security. As for the Chinese, they would like to have greater economic and trade ties with Burma.

"Not only is there is a fair amount of corruption among the SLORC leadership when it comes to drugs and arms, and a long history of human-rights abuse, there is also a long and tumultuous history between Burma and China."

* * *

When the Chinese Civil War broke out in 1949, fighting eventually spilled over onto Burmese territory. After Yunan Province in Southern China was taken over by the communist People's Liberation Army, the Nationalist (*Kuomintang*) forces crossed the border into Burma and began using the border areas as a base from which to attack the communist forces. By 1953, those Chi-

nese communist troops, called the Chinese Irregular Forces
(CIF), had entrenched themselves in Burma's Shan State, num-
bering as many as 12,000 men. But when the CIF realized that
they were out-numbered and out-armed by the Chinese Nationalist forces, they turned their attention from battling the communists to building up a profitable opium export business,
extending their control over most of the eastern portion of Shan
State. Before long, a "warlord" system developed and eventually
flourished, gradually extending into western Laos and northern
Thailand, creating what would be known as the Golden Triangle,
a major world center for opium cultivation and export.

In 1953, most of the Burmese Army was involved in fighting
the CIF, as well as battalions known as "Chinese irregu-
lars" that were also entrenched in the southern portion of the
Shan State. Although the Burmese Army launched numerous
offensives against the Chinese throughout that decade, the CIF
were never dislodged from their stronghold position in the Shan
State.

Despite historic tensions between Burma and China, the
fabled Burma Road—the old World War II route—remains Yun-
nan's best opening to the sea, and the main reason why China
has become one of Burma's principal allies and supplier of arms
to the current military regime. Access to the sea is the best
reason why China will never allow Burma to be isolated by
any international boycott—especially over human-rights abuses.
Although China and Burma are vastly different in natural
resources, population, and economic growth, they share a common fear that if either relinquishes power at the center of
the country, it will result in national disintegration. In Beijing
the argument is that if democracy ever succeeds, chaos will result in the form of secession of South China, Taiwan, Tibet, and
Sinkiang.

Armed with Chinese weapons, the SLORC is able to fight ethnic and narco rebels in Burma, either by reaching tenuous peace
accords or by guaranteeing them protection from other rene-
gade factions. To the east, India watches with a combination of

anxiety and interest, concerned over China's growing influence in Burma, which the Indians perceive as a threat to their own internal problems with Sikkh and other ethnic minorities. In the meantime, the SLORC has never forgotten the old Hindu belief that modern Burma is part of Greater India, causing Burma, throughout history, to consider China a tacit ally. There are many pundits, however, who disagree, judging China to be a greater threat to Burma's sovereignty than India. Some even predict that within the next twenty years China and India will wage war over Burma. It is a potential scenario that Asia would like to avoid at all costs.

According to Donald Keyser, China's main concern when it comes to Burma, and one which is periodically discussed in secret talks with the United States, has to do with narcotics coming out of that region. "As far as China is concerned and even India for that matter," Keyser says, "human-rights and democracy are the least of their concerns. The Chinese are concerned about the drug trade because it's beginning to affect their own people."

From a purely cynical point of view, Burma also represents for its Asian neighbors a new place to invest. For potential investors, money and political stability are far more important than installing an acceptable democratic regime in Rangoon that adheres to international standards of human-rights. Many international business people have politely suggested that "western liberals" look perhaps to Bosnia or Algeria, or India's victims in Kashmir and Punjab, and let Burma get on with business.

What is also certain is that an ethnically divided Burma would be an obvious *casus belli* between Asia's two superpowers, India and China. For Asia, a united Burma is better than a democratic Burma.

General Khin Nyunt, Secretary One of the SLORC, claims that the only reason certain countries threaten to impose economic sanctions on Burma is that the SLORC is not a democratic government. "They say that without a democratic government and stable situation, it is hard for the United States and other

European countries to invest in Myanmar," General Khin Nyunt maintains. "What I constantly tell them is to be patient and understand us, and to work together with us."

General David Abel, the affable Anglo-Burmese Minister of Foreign Trade, puts it another way when he says, "Any time an investor pulls out, there are many others who step in. You see, the cake is already baked. People are waiting to cut the cake and take a piece of it. I have told many American senators and congressmen that boycotts are not the way, you are too impatient and you are looking at things from an American perspective. You are not here and your presence here is absolutely necessary to understand our country. Not only is the American diplomatic presence needed, but also a commercial presence is imperative to understand how we operate."

*   *   *

Over the past ten years, the SLORC has changed in several very obvious ways. They are making attempts to become more sophisticated when it comes to dealing with the foreign press, as well as trying to placate various international human-rights groups by pretending to be willing to "escort visitors" around the country. As they told me in the very beginning of my visit, they wanted me to "see for myself all the progress the government has made for the people."

Recently, the regime has taken to giving weekly briefings for those journalists who are posted in Rangoon. They have also followed the example of The Burma Project and the NLD government-in-exile in Washington, D.C., by sending out information via the Internet. The contents of those press briefings and especially of those e-mails are mostly propaganda, limited to descriptions of SLORC generals inspecting bridges, railroads, bread factories, and other construction sites.

Only recently has CNN been permitted to install a satellite so that cable news can be seen in some of the more upscale hotels. Unfortunately, because access is so limited, and journalists are almost always prevented from coming into the country to inter-view the SLORC or The Lady, stock footage is used with regu-larity, accompanied by voice-over reports on any number of breaking news stories. Predictably, the SLORC seizes these examples of proof that, despite their willingness to be "more open," there is a western conspiracy bent on causing insurrec-tion throughout Burma. "Even the news uses old film because journalists don't want to admit that our country has vastly im-proved in the past few years," General Maung Maung maintains.

Another way that the SLORC has changed since Daw Suu Kyi has been liberated is to manifest a curious religious devotion. Hardly a day goes by without reports on the state television or in the state newspaper of SLORC generals dedicating newly constructed pagodas around the country. Unfortunately, the SLORC's born-again religious zealotry does not stop them from desecrating temples and burial grounds of religious minorities, such as Muslims and Christians. Of the SLORC's sudden devo-tion, Aung San Suu Kyi says, "I hope that they [the SLORC] will pay more attention to the essence of Buddhism. That would help a lot."

The SLORC responds to accusations of forced labor by claim-ing that it is in the Buddhist tradition for people to "donate" their time and efforts for the sake of building the country, as well as to earn merits for the next life. In the words of General Maung Maung, "There is an unwritten agreement with the people in the border areas, a cultural or national obligation, that the govern-ment will supply the material while the people will give their labor. Don't forget that our people are very strong Buddhists, which means that giving a helping hand to the army or to the community gains merits in our religion. Nobody forces the peo-ple to do anything. They volunteer."

General David Abel, the Anglo-Burmese official, agrees and offers the following insight, "It is the Asian way and one that has even been practiced in Europe. For instance, all the dikes in Hol-land were built by the Dutch for no money. And, following World War II in the United Kingdom, everybody went to work to reconstruct the country after the devastation caused by the bombings."

One afternoon I was taken by a government guide to the Tooth Relic Pagoda in Rangoon, currently in the process of being refurbished by the SLORC. Rows of people—men, women, and children, including soldiers—passed bags of sand, strips of wood, and other building materials from one to the other down a line that snaked around the pagoda and up a temporary wooden staircase to the dome. Inside the structure, artisans painted columns and retouched gold leaf on intricate designs, as well as polished the many statues of Buddha. Entire families had come to the pagoda to donate their time and efforts, some bringing their lunch and dinner, which were spread out on the marble floor throughout the immense room. My guide informed me that this was but one example of what the world called "forced labor," proof that there was a conspiracy to destroy the SLORC and to build up Aung San Suu Kyi.

What I saw at the Tooth Relic Pagado was not at all an example of what the world calls forced labor. The people who had traveled to the pagoda that day were fulfilling a duty in the Buddhist tradition where they give a certain number of hours to help others, or do good religious work to gain "merits" for their subsequent lives. What goes on in the border areas is quite another story.

What is so odd about the situation in Burma when it comes to the regime's human-rights record is that the Buddhist religion is against killing or harming any living being. Daw Suu Kyi offers the following insight into why countries such as Tibet, Cambodia, and Burma, with such large Buddhist populations, have so often had such violent rulers. "Sometimes I wonder," Daw Suu Kyi says, "if the countries that embraced Buddhism did so because they *needed* it, because there was something violent in their societies that *needed* to be controlled by Buddhism."

While the SLORC always justifies their actions by pulling out religious traditions, the Burmese people are either so frightened of repercussions, or too comfortable within the regime to risk their privileged positions, that it is difficult to learn just exactly what is going on throughout the country. To understand the suffering of the people, it's essential to see firsthand some of the abhorrent conditions that exist there.

On a subsequent trip to Burma, I entered the country through the Thai border. Upon my arrival, I was taken to one particular monastery where young men and women, infected with AIDS and obviously at the end of their lives, were lying on mattresses on the floor, waiting to die. When I interviewed a family whose fifteen-year-old daughter had contracted the virus after working in Bangkok as a prostitute, they explained through an interpreter, "Several businessmen came to our area and asked which girls wanted to go to Bangkok to work in a restaurant. My daughter wanted to go because we needed the money and, in our religion, it is an honor for children to help parents. She was gone for three years and we never had any news from her until we got a letter from a person we did not know who told us she was sick and was being sent home. When we welcomed her back, she was very thin and could hardly walk. In our village, there is no doctor but we took her to see a monk who brought a doctor in from another village. He said she had a virus and would probably die. Later on, we found out that she had worked in a house of prostitution in Bangkok."

A prominent woman scholar in Rangoon who works with women and children in the border areas confirmed what the young girl's father had told me. "It is considered an honor in the Buddhist religion for a child to bring money into the parents' home."

Asked if the parents know how their daughter will be earning money, "Yes," she admitted, "in most cases they do, but you must understand that as soon as our government can reach these rural areas by train or bridge, these young girls will have other alternatives to earn a living."

When I spoke to one of several monks who cares for people suffering from AIDS, he told me, again through an interpreter, that the young men and women in his charge are more fortunate than some. He suggested that I go with a colleague, who happened to be an ex-army officer, to several border villages. When we arrived at the first village, the ex-army officer pointed to a large area that he claimed was filled with mass graves where dozens of AIDS-infected Burmese had been shot and buried. While medical conditions in border areas are bad, and the military is often brutal, that would seem to be a gross exaggeration.

It is a grotesque equation: forced labor to build bridges and railroads that will ultimately save young women from fleeing across the border into Thailand where they work as prostitutes and often end up with AIDS.

Several days later I met with General Maung Maung once again. A deeply religious Buddhist, the general spent almost an entire evening with me talking about the joys of meditation. In the course of our meeting, I asked if young Burmese girls infected with HIV, after working in Thailand as prostitutes, were summarily executed on orders of the SLORC. "Those unfortunate girls are cared for by monks and doctors in clinics that we have recently built all along the border areas," the general answered. Shaking his head sadly, he added, "You know, it is against the Buddhist religion to kill anyone."

*   *   *

Another change in the SLORC since Daw Suu Kyi has been released is that they are providing her with soldiers who act as bodyguards, as well as drivers who chauffeur her whenever she is permitted outside her compound. General Khin Nyunt claims that The Lady requested security under the auspices of the SLORC, while Daw Suu Kyi claims that the SLORC offered it. "They would follow me anyway," she explains. "It just seemed simpler if they guarded the house and drove me."

While the world rejoiced that Aung San Suu Kyi was finally released, the reality is that she was actually liberated out of her house and into a larger prison, namely Rangoon. She is still unable to leave the country to visit friends and family in England, as she knows she would never be allowed back in to Burma, which would make her six-year incarceration meaningless.

There have been other subtle differences throughout the country in the last few years, both within the military regime and among various opposition groups. For instance, students, once linked solidly to Aung San Suu Kyi and the pro-democracy movement, have had several clashes with the authorities after which they have categorically denied any connection to the NLD or Aung San Suu Kyi.

According to "William," the prominent dissident who spent years in Insein Prison, most of the civilian population resent the students because the military and the police are more lenient with them because they fear mass rebellion within the cadre of the university. "The other reason for the distance is that the students know if they align themselves openly with the NLD, they will be treated as harshly."

* * *

In October 1996, while I was in Rangoon under the auspices of the SLORC, an incident occurred that many feared would be the beginning of another surge of violence as happened in 1988.

Once again, there was a knock on my door in the middle of the night. On that occasion, it was a foreign diplomat who told me there were riots going on, and suggested that it would be a good idea if I could witness the violence firsthand, and talk to some of the people involved. As it turned out, the diplomat was armed with a video camera that he managed to keep just below the car window to record the scene.

When the police finally understood what we were doing, they chased us away, but not before I had asked one what his orders were. Young, thin, and obviously terrified, the policeman replied, "We have orders to shoot to kill."

The incident began when three students, drunk and disorderly, ended up in a Rangoon bar that happened to be owned by the DDSI, or military intelligence. According to eyewitness reports, the students were rowdy. A fight broke out between the students and several customers over the music playing in the bar. Apparently, someone had changed a cassette tape without permission. The bartender managed to break up the fight before anyone got hurt, and threw the students out of the bar.

The trio left and wandered down the street for a while until suddenly deciding to go back to the bar to settle the score. Very drunk, the students strayed into the wrong bar and started shouting abuse, before realizing that the bar they wanted was several doors away. Staggering back, they entered the "right" bar and began throwing bottles around and overturning chairs. The owner managed to slip away unnoticed to call the police. When the police arrived, one of the students, wielding a broken bottle, lunged at a policeman, seriously cutting his eye. Later on, all the policemen at the scene would admit that they were not only scared because of the actual situation, but they were also fearful that the incident potentially could escalate into a student rally against the SLORC. As it turned out, they were right.

By the time we got there, students who were members of the Mandalay Club, a university organization, were demonstrating in front of the traffic light near Aung San Suu Kyi's house, which is only 150 yards from Yangon Institute of Technology. As my companion filmed, we watched the police try to control the crowd. Within minutes of our arrival, the police opened fire. I saw two students fall. When we got out of the car, it was obvious that one of the students was dead.

The following day, the government approached the student leaders in an effort to negotiate and quell the demonstrations before they spread throughout the entire city, and eventually the country. In response, the student leaders issued the following demands: The policemen who opened fire on the students would be brought to justice. The policemen must apologize. The incident must be reported truthfully in the local media. The students would not be harmed or prosecuted by the government. The SLORC must consider that the incident had nothing to do with politics but, rather, was only a student matter.

To understand the last condition, it is important to realize that every time there is an anti-SLORC demonstration, the regime systematically rounds up members of the NLD and hauls them off to prison. The students had included that last condition in an effort to protect the pro-democracy activists, including Aung San Suu Kyi, as well as to protect themselves from being linked to the NLD and suffering harsher punishment.

The following day, two government ministers arrived, one of whom was Dr. Khin Maung Nyunt, the Oxford-educated Deputy Minister of Education whom I had interviewed earlier, and who appeared relieved and willing to sign the agreement with the students. Later that day, Dr. Khin Maung Nyunt told me how pleased he was that the incident had nothing to do with the NLD or Aung San Suu Kyi. Based on the Deputy Minister's agreement and promise to uphold the conditions, the students promised that calm would be restored within the university.

The following day, however, *The New Light of Myanmar* ran an article that claimed that only one student had been stabbed. Further, the article stated that when the police arrived, they had no idea that the perpetrators were students, nor did they understand that the riots that followed were caused by students. The inference was that had the police been aware that the trio in the bar were students (if, for example, the police had checked their identity cards) they never would have responded so violently by opening fire into the crowd.

The reaction from the students was predictable.

The SLORC had broken their promise.

The SLORC had lied by protecting the policeman.

As one Burmese pro-democracy leader said, "The SLORC could have protected all the police by sacrificing the ones who had opened fire. At least for the sake of restoring peace and quiet among the student population, they should have kept to the agreement."

A mass meeting was called at the university, which eventually brought students from universities in other cities, all of whom were united in their accusations of police brutality. Finally, at five o'clock the following morning, the meeting broke up and the students dispersed, having already agreed to stage a big rally later that day. Predictably, troops were called in and the entire area was cordoned off.

Several hours before the rally was to take place, two university students went unannounced to U Kyi Maung's house—out of courtesy—to inform Daw Suu Kyi's close colleague what was going on. According to U Kyi Maung, during the visit, the students also told him that the body of the student who had been killed was now missing. Apparently the police had simply taken the young man's body to avoid more violence, claiming that he was being held at a police station for questioning. As a result of the students' visit to U Kyi Maung, however, the NLD leader was arrested and held at a "government guest house" for questioning concerning his involvement in "instigating riots and demonstrations against the government."

Eventually, U Kyi Maung was released. Following the incident, I interviewed a lieutenant colonel attached to the SLORC who had been put in charge of controlling the violence during the three-day uprising. The only point that he insisted on making during the interview was that any anti-SLORC demonstrations that break out sporadically throughout the university are independent of the NLD and Aung San Suu Kyi.

"But if that is the case, why was U Kyi Maung detained?" I asked.

"He was not detained. He was invited to talk to some government officials to give his opinion on maintaining law and order."

It occurred to me that during the Gulf War, Saddam Hussein had referred to the hostages as "guests."

"Sometimes the students demonstrate for things that have only to do with university life," the Lieutenant Colonel continued. "But the NLD uses the student unrest as an example that they also are filled with anti-government sentiment. The truth is the NLD has lost a lot of its power, especially within the university."

I asked where the student was that everyone believes is dead?

"At the police station, sleeping it off." I then asked, "Why don't you put him on television so the people can see that he is alive?"

At that point, the Lieutenant Colonel ended the interview.

Several hours later, foreign diplomats from the American and British embassies demanded that the SLORC produce the student who was allegedly being held at a police station to satisfy not only his family, but the entire country, who were convinced that he had been killed.

The SLORC refused.

By then, the area around the university and on University Avenue near Aung San Suu Kyi's house was closed, and guarded by soldiers.

The streets were once again calm.

The missing student remained missing.

Later on, I learned that his family had begged the authorities for his body so they could give him a proper funeral.

Several evenings later, I was invited to dinner with General Maung Maung and his wife, along with the foreign diplomat who had taken me along to watch the riots while he videotaped them. Predictably, the conversation turned to the events of the previous several days. General Maung Maung offered his opinion. "The big mistake was that the police never should have beaten those students in front of witnesses."

After dinner, on the way home in his bullet-proof car, the foreign diplomat confessed that when General Maung Maung made that comment during dinner, he dared not look at me from across the table.

21

IN TYPICAL SLORC contradiction, while trying to distance the student demonstrations from the NLD, whenever there are any demonstrations the regime automatically blames NLD leaders for instigating them. It is the regime's way of keeping the focus of government opposition only on Aung San Suu Kyi and her pro-democracy party. For instance, in the winter of 1997 in Rangoon, students demonstrated at Yangon Institute of Technology, demanding that the government allow them to form student unions. The SLORC's immediate response was to arrest more than twenty-five NLD activists and remand them to Insein Prison.

There are many foreign diplomats in Rangoon who believe that the SLORC wants to give the impression that the only group that is opposed to the regime is the NLD, led by Aung San Suu Kyi.

The situation in Burma continues to be not only unstable and often violent, but it is increasingly more complicated, since there are no longer only two opposing camps. What was once an easily distinguishable question of good versus evil in Burma has now become a matter of which group can offer the people the most appealing promises. It is a situation that can only get worse. The worse it gets, the more the Burmese people will suffer.

Despite the increasing control the SLORC has over the population, it is apparent that they are nonetheless feeling international pressure. Lately, there is a note of desperation in their propaganda.

In December 1996, a bomb went off at the SLORC's Tooth Relic Pagoda, injuring seventeen people and killing three. The SLORC immediately accused the NLD.

On April 7, 1997, the letter bomb that exploded at General Tin Oo's house and killed his daughter immediately set off a renewed security alert throughout the capital. Government officials claimed that the bomb had been mailed from Japan on the orders of NLD pro-democracy activists in Burma. Blaming the NLD was a predictable SLORC reaction, which prompted Aung San Suu Kyi not only to deny any involvement in the attack, but to call for international intervention to protect members of her pro-democracy movement from government reprisals.

Several western diplomats stationed in Rangoon, as well as a high-placed Asian businessman, all agreed that the letter bomb sent to General Tin Oo only supported what had been rumored around the country for months. According to those same sources, and to several SLORC advisors with whom I spoke, there is a serious rupture within the SLORC ranks. Contact has already been successfully made with more moderate factions within the SLORC, and General Tin Oo was known to be a hardliner who was against any negotiation or reconcilliation with Aung San Suu Kyi and her National League for Democracy followers.

On June 9, 1997, during one of their weekly press conferences in Rangoon, the SLORC exhibited what they claimed were seized documents that linked Washington to terrorist plots against the military regime.

Several military intelligence officers showed what they claimed was a photocopy of a list of United States government foreign appropriations. Under the heading "Burma," the list included more than $2.3 million earmarked for Burmese student groups who supported the pro-democracy movement. According to one of the intelligence officers, Colonel Thein Swe, the money was brought into Burma across the Thai-Burmese border. Further, General Khin Nyunt accused Washington of financing pro-democracy activities, including supporting Aung San Suu Kyi's NLD, who, the general said, were planning a series of bombings in Rangoon.

While Washington and the NLD denied the accusations, the SLORC produced other documents that purported to prove that cash transfers from the United States–based Asian American Federation of Labor Institute had reached Aung San Suu Kyi in Rangoon.

Obviously, the SLORC is forced to accuse The Lady, the pro-democracy movement, and the United States, which is clearly against the regime. Despite all the contradictions that are inherent throughout Burmese politics, and notwithstanding any rumors about rifts within the regime itself, the issues facing Burma today are not clearly black and white. For the purpose of deciphering fact from fiction, it is important to understand that throughout Burmese history, the same internal conflicts have repeated themselves. Unresolved, these conflicts have doomed the Burmese people to endure chaos, violence, deception, and a series of brutal regimes for generations. What makes this political situation different from all the others, however, is the constant pressure put on the SLORC by Aung San Suu Kyi and her colleagues in the NLD.

There is no doubt that Daw Suu Kyi is brave. Taking a vocal stand against a military regime that does not adhere to international law is indeed act of courage. There is also no doubt that Daw Suu Kyi appeared in Rangoon at a time when there was a real chance for political change, and that she succeeded in creating a voice for the people after decades of collective silence. "What is remarkable about Suu," a British journalist says, "is her grasp of Burmese politics. Many people have good ideas for Burma but they're not in Burma, and once you're out, you don't get back in. Suu is there and she won't leave."

Without the voice and person of Aung San Suu Kyi, the world would have remained ignorant of the political situation in

Burma. "You need an activist to take a legitimate cause and make it a legitimate policy," a Washington, D.C., activist for human-rights contends. "And with this kind of rapacious regime in Rangoon there are no cameras or journalists allowed in to record the atrocities. All the people have is this stellar lady sitting in her house on Inya Lake."

The result of the growing political opposition to the SLORC and the media coverage of Aung San Suu Kyi, the regime is now forced to take into account international reaction to their practices.

Another Washington activist involved in bringing human-rights and democracy to Burma says, "In Burma, time is on the side of the oppressor. If you're hungry, one day more makes a big difference in your life. If you're being raped, one minute more makes a big difference in your life. If you're being forcibly relocated from your home to make room for a railroad or a gas pipeline, never to return, one week is a long time. It's always the victim who loses in the time game and the SLORC understands that only too well."

Aung San Suu Kyi has repeatedly called for international investment to be linked to human-rights provisions.

The Association of South East Asian Nations, or ASEAN, has taken a consistent position that "constructive engagement" is the only way to facilitate change within the SLORC ultimately to satisfy western standards of democracy and human-rights.

Yet another Washington lobbyist for human-rights in Burma claims that it is impossible to ever change ASEAN's position when it comes to Burma. "ASEAN is completely wrong," the activist says, "if they believe that engagement with the SLORC will make them see the light. Imagine if SLORC goes to the other countries in the neighborhood who are members of ASEAN— like Indonesia or Singapore, for instance—and asks them advice about turning over power to a Buddhist nonviolent woman who also just happens to have won the Nobel Peace Prize. What do you think their response will be? Obviously, they're not going to encourage the SLORC to step down because the next thing you know the people of East Timor and Indonesia will be making the same demands. As a matter of fact, there's a woman running around Indonesia right now using the D-word. Basically, the advice ASEAN is going to give the SLORC is to go right back home and order new weapons from China because the last thing any of those countries wants is an epidemic of democracy in that part of the world."

For years, Aung San Suu Kyi has taken the position that any international aid given to Burma, or any international investment made in the country, only helps to keep the SLORC in power. "I think all international opinion counts," she says. "In this day and age any government cannot be oblivious to international opinion, and international action will certainly have some kind of effect. Exactly what sort of effect is difficult to say, because we are so close to events. I think it is only after about ten or fifteen years when we are further away from events and we know more about what went on inside the inner circle of the administration that we'll be able to decide definitely how much effect sanctions had. In the beginning we did not call for international sanctions but we now endorse the idea because we have come to the conclusion that investments in Burma have not in any way helped the people nor helped the course of democracy. Our main worry about sanctions previously was that they might harm the people of Burma, that they might have adverse effects on the public at large. But we have come to the conclusion that investments in Burma have so far not benefited the majority of the people."

When I was in Rangoon, I made a tour one evening of the many brand-new hotels that had recently opened in anticipation of "Visit Myanmar Year" in 1996. With the exception of housing several groups of German tourists and a handful of Japanese businessmen, the hotels were empty, the discos were silent, and the vast parking lots were filled only with cab drivers sitting on the pavement playing cards. Walking through one cavernous lobby after the other, I spoke to waiters, desk clerks, and maitre d's, who all said that the longer the hotels remained empty, the more likely they were to lose their jobs. As that Washington activist pointed out, "In the short-term, the waiting game is always harder on the victim."

In a study conducted by Professor Daniel Bradlow on International Financial Institutions, and published in conjunction with a paper on *The World Bank, Human Rights, Democracy, and Governance: Burma, A Case Study* by Nicholas H. Moller, the suggestion of a compromise is discussed in which western countries would continue to take a tough stand when it comes to the SLORC and human-rights issues, while ASEAN would take a position less severe in order to ensure the eventuality of a dialogue.

In response, Daw Suu Kyi says, "The SLORC cannot maintain the current level of economic development without thinking of the welfare of the people. Only a few in the society benefit, while the more fortunate citizens who try to invest find themselves denied necessary permits because opportunities are given to those better connected. What's more, long-term prospects for the economy are greatly weakened by the havoc wreaked on the education system by the SLORC. The government is stifling education, and education is the key to the economy. But what is even worse is that thousands of people are used to build up the country in such inhuman conditions that they usually die from their efforts."

Those who work closely with Daw Suu Kyi believe that despite her initial political inexperience and the fact that she lived almost her entire life abroad, she has nonetheless grown into the role of a seasoned *de facto* opposition leader. U Kyi Maung, her close colleague, says, "She is committed to the cause of multi-party democracy, and has become very aware of subversive groups that have tried to use her name and image."

Maureen Aung-Thwin, who runs George Soros' Burma Project in New York, says of Aung San Suu Kyi, "Although Suu initiall lacked a defined political platform for her nonviolent stand, she is now the single greatest threat to military rule. And, regardless of which groups are anti-SLORC and claim to be separate from Suu Kyi, the fact remains that the government considers Suu to be the symbol of opposition."

Journalists and diplomats who have observed Daw Suu Kyi since 1988 agree that she has changed from a giggling and inexperienced public speaker to a woman who appears to take the fate of the Burmese people seriously. Yet, many of those same journalists and writers who have interviewed her also claim that she has not learned to separate her personal identity from her political image. According to several, The Lady takes umbrage if she is challenged on any specific issue or position. She becomes haughty, they say, retreating behind an academic snobbism that tends to intimidate and discourage people from approaching her. A journalist from *Time* magazine recalls that when she asked a question that Daw Suu Kyi perceived to be challenging, her response was to rise and exit. "One of her aides came in and just announced that The Lady had a previous appointment," the journalist says, "and the interview was over."

Another western observer disagrees, however, and offers the following insight on Aung San Suu Kyi's political image. "When people talk about the individual, negative comments come out. People say that Suu has a reputation for being haughty. So what? That's the nature of the game and it shouldn't be seen as putting Suu down. After all, world leaders are a strange breed. Her supporters should stop creating the image that she is Saint Suu because it's detrimental in the long run for the cause. The point is not to create a demagogue but to further democracy."

One of the major problems is that Aung San Suu Kyi's supporters, mainly outside Burma, have done just that.

Often, if a journalist or a diplomat, a Burmese scholar, or a politician criticizes Daw Suu Kyi, her supporters are apt to consider it tantamount to opposing the pro-democracy movement in Burma. Those people who are interested in Daw Suu Kyi as well as the overall political situation in Burma, whether they are writing articles or books or are students engaged in academic research, discover very quickly that there are precise rules that must be followed. If not, information and interviews are difficult to obtain. The conditions are simple.

Any involvement or comment concerning the Burmese struggle for democracy should include only a condemnation of the SLORC. Deconstructing Aung San Suu Kyi is not part of the game.

In their own defense, certain of Daw Suu Kyi's supporters insist that she has achieved so much for the Burmese people in so short a time, and under such extraordinarily difficult circumstances, that even the slightest negative comment or opinion is immediately used as negative propaganda by the SLORC. Unfortunately, they are right, although it does not solve the problem, nor does it make Aung San Suu Kyi and the pro-democracy movement more accessible to everyone.

As for the SLORC and their way of handling the political situation in Burma, or criticism from within the country, as well as from the international community, their problems are more serious.

On my last day in Rangoon, I was taken by several members of the SLORC to visit a nun who, according to my hosts, was the most accurate purveyor of the future in the country. In fact, she had the distinction of being known as the fortune-teller to the SLORC.

An obviously kind woman in her fifties, with muscular arms and legs, thick glasses that magnified her black eyes, and her head shaved in Buddhist tradition, the nun runs an orphanage on the outskirts of Rangoon. A large gothic structure, the orphanage is surrounded by shrines and small pagodas, gardens, pebble driveways and walkways, and terraces that wrap around the entire building. Inside, there are several large dormitory rooms with cots lining each wall where the children sleep. In exchange for private donations and a monthly stipend from the government that feeds and clothes the children, the nun limits her spiritual advice and guidance to members of the SLORC, or SLORC friends and family.

Sitting cross-legged on the floor in a vast room where there was an array of antiques, jeweled shrines, and golden Buddhas, the nun dealt patiently with the questions of the two military men concerning politics, before answering my queries concerning life, love, and career. In perhaps the most stunning example of just how inculcated mysticism and spiritualism are in the Burmese psyche, my two SLORC companions actually questioned the nun on the political future of Aung San Suu Kyi, asking advice on how the government should deal with demonstrations and general opposition to the government.

Months after I left Rangoon, I received a telephone call from one of the military men present that day, who inquired if the nun's predictions for me had come true. When I responded that I barely remembered my questions or her answers, he reminded me that the nun had predicted that Burma would be granted membership into ASEAN toward the middle of 1997. He was pleased to point out that once again the nun was correct. Burma, in fact, was accorded full membership standing in ASEAN during the summer of 1997.

22

Most revolutions or political movements have different leaders for different stages of their struggles. For example, another woman who gained prominence in the beginning of a national crusade was Hanan Ashrawi, the spokesperson for the Palestinian Liberation Organization. During the initial phases of the Middle East Peace Conference held in Madrid, and the latter stages of the conference that took place in Washington before culminating in Oslo where the peace agreement was signed, Hanan succeeded in changing the image of the PLO from a terrorist organization to a bonafide revolutionary movement. Yet, in the end, she never reached the heights expected of her after the historic handshake on the White House lawn between Yitzak Rabin and Yasser Arafat.

Aung San Suu Kyi is pragmatic enough to admit that the needs of the people and the country will undoubtedly change as time passes. "I don't think I will let the people down," she says, "although I don't believe that I will be able to do everything they want. But I have never promised them anything. I simply said I would try my best right now."

More than doing her best, even after having won the election, it is clear that Daw Suu Kyi is willing to negotiate certain points with the SLORC, such as who should ultimately govern Burma, and how much power the military should have.

In order for the SLORC to agree to return to the barracks and honor the results of another democratic election, they must first reject Item 6, which they have already written into the new constitution, and which states that the "military is entitled to one-fourth the power in the parliament."

It doesn't seem very likely, since only recently the SLORC has composed yet another slogan, which they call "Declaration 1."

Displayed on freshly painted billboards throughout Rangoon are the regime's four national objectives: peace, tranquility, and security to build a nation; free-market economy; multiparty democratic system after a new constitution is drafted; and national unity.

"If you analyze every one of these four objectives," General Khin Nyunt explains, "it's obvious that the SLORC wants what is best for the people. It is also obvious that the armed forces are not here to govern forever."

George Orwell served in Burma as a British colonial police officer in the 1920s. The observation that he made about the country and the government more than seventy years ago is still relevant. "In Burma," Orwell said, "the past belongs to those who control the present."

Afterword

After nineteen months of house arrest, Aung San Suu Kyi was released on May 6, 2002, by Burma's military regime. The world hoped that her release was unconditional, meaning she could hold political meetings, address the crowds of supporters that gathered in front of her lakeside house every week, travel without restriction, and receive the foreign diplomats and human rights activists who depend on her for truthful reports about conditions in Burma. Not surprisingly, given the duplicity and brutality of the military junta, her release was not what she and the thousands who had supported her throughout this latest ordeal had hoped for. During a recent interview from her home on Inya Lake, Aung San Suu Kyi said, "I'm not under house arrest again, but my movements are quite restricted. And the movements of those who wish to come and see me are restricted. So it's quite obvious that the SLORC is very nervous about what the NLD is capable of doing. If they were not nervous about the strength of the NLD, they wouldn't impose these restrictions. They know that we are a powerful force within the country."

The SLORC's peculiar interpretation of liberty, freedom, and unconditional release is an old story. In fact, nothing much has changed in Burma since the military junta took power illegally in 1988, except their name. Perhaps one of the many

American public relations firms who have represented the junta in an effort to clean up its reputation, or one of the numerous foreign investors who have made a fortune by using forced Burmese labor and benefiting from dubious tax benefits, revealed that the State Law and Order Restoration Council, or SLORC, had become the butt of jokes throughout the civilized world. After fourteen years of operating under that name, a perfect onomatopoeic acronym for them, they opted to change it to the State Peace and Development Council. There are few other than those whose business interests depend on the SLORC's survival who refer to them as the SPDC.

After fourteen years in power, the SLORC remains just as naive and stubborn about courting international favor or understanding the human rights standards that govern much of this twenty-first-century world as they were when they started out. They are still a Disneyland of juntas, with ersatz military men who wear rimless sunglasses and white gloves and whose khaki shirts are covered with colored ribbons and medals, the usual accessories of the brutal and corrupt—or, in their case, a visual example of a combination of Stalinist regime, South American fascist junta, and twisted version of self-indulgent capitalism. When accused in a recent telephone interview that the government still controls the press, for example, an advisor to General Khin Nyunt simply and dismissively replied, "The contents of all government meetings or appearances of the top generals are recounted in minutes which are published in our newspaper," as if that were all it took to establish a free press.

When the key players in the SLORC make appearances, the occasion is usually the release of a commemorative book that has to do with the military's imagined feats during the last forty or so years. During that same phone interview, General Khin Nyunt's advisor recounted a typical day for one of the top military officials. "There are a good many goodwill delegations," he said proudly. "We are in close touch with the people."

Those "goodwill" delegations are almost always accompanied by a twenty-one gun salute, forced cheers from crowds who are bussed in and photographed waving miniature Burmese flags, and little girls offering bouquets to Secretary One or Senior General Two. There are many "official ceremonies" as well, such as ribbon cuttings or inspections of vegetable shops, fish and egg markets, edible oil and rice boutiques, and tax-free markets. What there aren't are military parades with the prerequisite display of arms, since this junta is not strong in high-tech military hardware. Their strength is in the fear they have instilled throughout the society, where people, including children, denounce their parents, friends, teachers, and anyone else who dares to utter a dissenting opinion or take part in a demonstration against the government.

The government meetings that are reported in meticulous and agonizing detail—including every cough and sneeze—cover entertainment groups, transport associations, photo displays, and round-table discussions which, according to the same government advisor, involve "scrutinizing" committees who decide on literary and art prizes ranging from the best translation to the most intricate tapestry. "One meeting was especially tedious," the government advisor explained, "because there was a discussion about the size of the photograph that must accompany each application." If the result of this ridiculous display of so-called transparency—openness about meaningless meetings—did not have such dire consequences for the Burmese people, the situation would make for brilliant political satire.

The more serious charges against the SLORC, however, are not their narcissism or their inflated opinion of themselves, but rather their disregard for the poverty that is rampant throughout the country (except among the high-ranking military leaders and their close friends), a growing government deficit, rising inflation, and shortages in energy supplies (brownouts and blackouts occur more frequently than ever before owing to the influx of foreign companies who have brought with them energy-guzzling high-tech computers and other modern equipment).

The most reprehensible charges are the SLORC's abuses of

power in arresting and imprisoning citizens without trial, their disrespect for human rights, and their unconscionable collusion with drug lords who ultimately supply heroin and methamphetamine drugs throughout the world. There is still no adequate program against the rising AIDS epidemic in Burma, which continues to take a backseat to the military, the government's first priority. The military budget is more than 60 percent of all other spending, yet it is used to finance the junta's opulent lifestyle rather than to buy modern equipment.

Fortunately for the Burmese people, the generals have no concept of political nuance, which makes it virtually impossible for them to fool the rest of the world.

Fortunately for the rest of the world, so far even the most cynical terror groups consider the generals too unreliable to approach about setting up training camps in return for vast financial rewards.

Much like their predecessor and now disgraced former dictator, Ne Win, who isolated Burma from the rest of the world for decades, the generals continue to view things through their own highly subjective prism. The result is that they not only refuse to sit down and negotiate with the many ethnic minorities that are a legitimate and important part of the population, but they have unleashed their army along the northern border with Thailand as a way of deflecting the promise that they made to the international community: to start serious discussions with the National League for Democracy Party, which would lead to a civilian regime led by the party that legitimately won the people's vote in 1990.

After three lengthy house arrests, Aung San Suu Kyi is still battling with the dictatorship for a dialogue that would lead to her rightful place at the head of the government. Her commitment to her cause of freedom for the Burmese people was never more starkly illustrated than in 1999 when her husband, Michael Aris, still living in the United Kingdom, was terminally ill with prostate cancer. By that time, she had not seen him for three years, and although the junta offered her a visa to visit her dying husband, Aung San Suu Kyi refused, knowing that she would be blocked from ever returning to Burma to continue her political struggle. As a result, she was denied a final reunion before he died in March 1999.

Immediately upon Aung San Suu Kyi's release from house arrest this past May, there was speculation that she might soften certain of her party's demands on the military in return for opening a dialogue which would lead to political reconciliation. Instead, and much to the relief of the general population and international observers, she not only restated, on behalf of her party, a demand that the ruling junta acknowledge her 1990 election victory, but she also asked for the release of all political prisoners being held illegally. On May 14, 2002, nine members of the NLD were released, although Amnesty International claimed there were at least fifteen hundred more languishing in Burmese jails. In response, the junta asserted that those in custody were either common criminals or terrorists, or had been arrested because of acts of insurgency against the government.

In Burma, if more than two people meet in a coffee shop, they can be accused of plotting a coup.

On the morning of May 27, Aung San Suu Kyi went even further in her determination to confront the junta by announcing that she intended to start an opposition newspaper— a bold statement considering that the authorities keep such strict controls on all the country's newspapers and electronic media that they are nothing more than a platform for government propaganda. On the evening of May 27, Aung San Suu Kyi united all the elected representatives, including diplomats from Britain, France, Italy, Germany, South Korea, Japan, Australia, and the United States, in a twelfth anniversary celebration of their victory at party headquarters in Rangoon. During the ceremony, a senior member of the NLD read the following statement: "The only means to deal with the results of the 1990 election and the prevailing political, economic, social, health, and educational matters is a meaningful dialogue . . . And

through this dialogue, a parliament with the elected representatives of the 1990 elections must be convened to establish a
democratic country."

The subtext of that statement did not elude the SLORC.

The task of writing the constitution that would be the basis
for a new parliament has not progressed since my last visit to
Burma, in 1997. At the time, SLORC government officials took
me to visit some of the "parliamentary committees" that were,
they claimed, in the process of writing a new constitution—
which was as invisible as the emperor's new clothes. The reality
is that while the process of organizing committees to work on
separate specially assigned topics of this constitution began in
1993, there has been no progress since 1996. The only sign of
any forward movement was in October 2000, when Aung San
Suu Kyi was called in for secret negotiations with the military
concerning the constitutional process and a transition to an
open-market democracy. Once again, the talks brought no results. During my telephone interview with her after her latest
release, Aung San Suu Kyi commented on the process of writing a new constitution, the key to change in the government. "I
think the real trouble with the National Convention," she said,
"is that it is not really a National Convention. A genuine National Convention must be one made up of people who have
been elected or selected by the public in some way or the other,
which is not the case of this present Convention. That is its
main trouble."

During recent interviews with several SLORC government
officials, it became clear that the new constitution is not finished—which, according to them, means that the country does
not have a basis of law and order that would permit citizens to
understand "the laws, which in turn would set down the rules
by which elections should be held." One Western diplomat who
is now stationed in Rangoon laughed when he was asked to
comment on the seemingly endless process that the military
government is going through as a prologue to the democratic
process they have been promising for more than two decades.
"At this rate, which seems to be that they are writing one sen-

tence a year and not even in final draft," he said, "we'll all be dead and our children and grandchildren will be dead by the time this constitution is finished."

If Aung San Suu Kyi's freedom was not without conditions, it was also not without certain financial implications, whose benefits for the Burmese people are at best unclear. For example, immediately upon her release, Japan resumed its official development assistance program and announced that it was giving $5 million toward the renovation of a Burmese power plant. While in principle that should help the non-SLORC Burmese, it remains doubtful that any financial aid will actually reach its designated goal. In fact, it is more likely that any monies will end up in the coffers of the military regime. The most questionable arrangement or reward for Aung San Suu Kyi's release, however, was a business deal that indirectly involved President George W. Bush.

In April 2002, the SLORC hired a Washington-based public relations firm, DCI Associates, headed by Thomas J. Synhorst, a well-known Republican lobbyist with close ties to President Bush and the tobacco industry. Synhorst, who specializes in mobilizing support for his clients through the extensive use of telephone contact, signed a contract with the junta that gave him an annual retainer of $450,000 per year with an initial deposit upon signature of $100,000. The conditions for the deposit were predicated on the release of Aung San Suu Kyi from house arrest. According to several government opposition sources in Burma, the junta believed that this contact would eventually lead the United States to lift economic sanctions against them. So far, however, the Bush administration has given only $1 million in humanitarian aid through several United Nations agencies and other nongovernmental organizations in Burma, to assist in battling an HIV epidemic that affects one out of every fifty adults. While the AIDS rate is one of the highest in the world, Burma's official budget to combat the disease in 1999 was $30,000, supplemented by about $3 million from international organizations.

As usual, the amount of humanitarian aid that reaches the

people is grossly inadequate. "Inflation is rampant," Aung San Suu Kyi explained during that same recent interview, "and the economy is going downhill. There isn't a kind of accountable, transparent government that is necessary to make an economic success out of an open-market system, and economics and politics are interminably connected. If the government is unable to cope with the economy, there is bound to be a push for political change."

Various figures representing international organizations who return from visiting Burma insist that the SLORC is "destined for change." The United Nations special rapporteur on human rights, Paulo Sergio Pinheiro, made a statement in Geneva recently about the necessity for the European Community to change its tactics toward Burma and support the efforts of the United Nations. The message was clear: If the European Community expected and desired to see political and human rights progress, they should support a spirit of "principled engagement." He added that while the process was "slow with limited political results," he continues to believe that there is a "will within the SLORC" to change and to "pursue a transition from political exclusion to cooperation with the National League for Democracy Party and other components of society."

Mr. Pinheiro went on to praise the military junta for releasing more than 263 detainees over the prior fifteen months, though he did not bother to discuss the absence of a democratic process and fair trial system that had resulted in these people having been arrested in the first place—most for their involvement with the NLD, or because they attempted to meet with others, or simply because they were caught passing out pamphlets calling for democracy. Perhaps the only concrete effort that helped to assure Aung San Suu Kyi's release was the visit by Kofi Anan's special envoy, Ismail Razali, to Burma during its New Year festival in April, when he expressed the hope that it was the right time of year for leaders to make gestures that respect international human rights standards and point to a desire to implement a democracy that would include respect for the people's choice during the last election, and thus the right time to usher in a new era of development for the country.

And yet, notwithstanding Aung San Suu Kyi's release from house arrest, the situation in Burma is tenuous and fraught with contradiction.

Does Aung San Suu Kyi's freedom mean that the military government will allow her to conduct political meetings and rallies to mobilize the people to take over the country as was ordained when the NLD won the elections in 1990?

Does her freedom mean that a responsible and serious dialogue will open between the NLD and the military junta?

Does her freedom mean that the more than fifteen hundred political detainees who are languishing in abhorrent conditions in Burmese jails will be released?

Does her freedom include a tripartite dialogue between the military, the NLD, and the ethnic minorities who must have a strong voice in a new government?

And finally, does Aung San Suu Kyi's freedom mean that she can finally take her place as head of the National League for Democracy Party and lead the Burmese people into an enlightened and free existence?

Based on history, the prospect is not encouraging.

Based on the indomitable will and personal sacrifices that Aung San Suu Kyi has made for the Burmese people, there is hope.

"I have said I am a cautious optimist," Aung San Suu Kyi said shortly after her release. "Nothing has ever happened to make me change my mind. My view is that when you set out to achieve something you don't just depend on hope, you put in a lot of hard work."

Based on her words, a democratic future for the Burmese people seems assured.

—Barbara Victor, June 2002